When Your Child
Learns *Differently*

A Family Approach for Navigating
Special Education Services
With Love and High Expectations

Kathryn Fishman-Weaver, Ph.D.

PRUFROCK PRESS INC.
WACO, TEXAS

Library of Congress catalog information
currently on file with the publisher.

Copyright ©2019, Prufrock Press Inc.

Edited by Stephanie McCauley

Cover and layout design by Allegra Denbo

ISBN-13: 978-1-61821-909-1

Printed in the United States of America.

At the time of this book's publication, all facts and figures cited are the most current available.
All telephone numbers, addresses, and website URLs are accurate and active. All publica-
tions, organizations, websites, and other resources exist as described in the book, and all have
been verified. The author and Prufrock Press Inc. make no warranty or guarantee concerning
the information and materials given out by organizations or content found at websites, and
we are not responsible for any changes that occur after this book's publication. If you find an
error, please contact Prufrock Press Inc.

Prufrock Press Inc.
P.O. Box 8813
Waco, TX 76714-8813
Phone: (800) 998-2208
Fax: (800) 240-0333
http://www.prufrock.com

Dedication

This book is dedicated to my students' families who taught me the power of high expectations, the importance of advocacy, and that love is the most important force in helping children succeed.

Table of Contents

Acknowledgments

This book exists because a group of extraordinary first-grade students taught me how to be a teacher. The sunny classroom I shared with those children forever shaped who I am as an educator, parent, and human being. Throughout these pages, I can hear the voices of Gah-mel's auntie, Isaac's grandmother, Christian's parents, Ana's mom, Demarco's grandmother, Brad's dad, Luiza's mom, and Esperanza's aunt[1]. These families showed me that with love and high expectations, almost anything is possible. I also am indebted to Ms. Tonnesha Pace, my brilliant partner in caring for and teaching that first groups of students. Not only did she help me become a better teacher, but she also supported me with friendship and guidance when I was a brand-new mother.

My husband Chris willed this book into being by encouraging me that this was "a book I had to write." He said it often enough that, finally, I had no choice but to agree. Our children (especially our son) helped to bring this book into being. As I was writing *When Your Child Learns Differently*, our son was right there. I thought of him as a second grader who loved to kick soccer balls over the fence, as a fifth grader who fell in love with reading *Harry Potter*, as a seventh grader riding his bike to middle school, as a ninth grader who broke my heart when he gave up the clarinet, and as an eleventh grader who became a track star. He now towers above me at 6'3" and is finding his way post high school graduation.

I have a wonderful group of family and friends who were the recipients of endless frantic text messages about this project. These people came

---

1 Most of the student names used in this book are pseudonyms. Although their identifying information belongs to them, these stories are a gift to us all.

to editing parties, met me for lunch, picked me up (figuratively and literally) when I was feeling discouraged, and reminded me that they believed this project was important and that I was the right person to write it. Their support kept me going. Thank you especially to Gloria and Lenny Fishman, Julie Harpring, Chris Holmes, Teri Walden, Danielle McAfee-Thoenen, Stephanie Walter, Jill Clingan, Lisa DeCastro, Katherine Sasser, Matt Miltenberg, and Rachel Harper. I'm sorry for the late night and early morning messages, and I appreciate that you always responded with compassion and enthusiasm.

Thank you again to Stephanie McCauley, Joel McIntosh, and all of the encouraging people at Prufrock Press who said that even though this book was a completely new project, they believed in it, too, and wanted to help me nurture it to publication. Prufrock Press is doing important work celebrating the idiosyncrasies of children who learn differently, and I'm proud to have this second title with them.

While working on *When Your Child Learns Differently*, I talked with countless families who heard about the project and offered their stories and worries candidly and vulnerably. These stories were a gift that encouraged me to keep writing. They reminded me that

› parenting is hard and beautiful,
› all families are still figuring it out, and
› we don't talk about these truths enough.

To everyone who shared their stories of raising, loving, and believing in children who learn differently, thank you!

About the Cover Image

One panel of "The Peace Mural," created by students from ASCEND K–8 School, Oakland, CA, 2008.

I have an old pair of paint-splattered jeans in the back of my closet. Although they're ruined, I can't bring myself to let them go. (Yes, it's possible that I hold onto things too tightly.) It was spring of 2008—a perfect day for painting outside with an enthusiastic group of 6- and 7-year-olds. We were working together on "The Peace Mural" shown on this book's cover.

If you happened to walk by that day, you might have heard the occasional measure of one of those random songs that sometimes escape when young children are hard at work. You probably would have smiled at the sweet group of friends painting together on a bright, breezy day. You wouldn't, however, have known that one fifth of the first and second graders working on this project had disabilities. You also wouldn't know that this was the first of several large-scale inclusive learning expeditions we would complete together at this K–8 public school in Oakland, CA.

During this particular learning expedition on nonviolence, our classes recorded a CD of peace songs and created "The Peace Mural." This mural was orchestrated under the artistic direction of Miranda Bergman and completed by the first- and second-grade students in my self-contained early-elementary group, in collaboration with Lisa DeCastro's and Ashley English's first-grade classes. Our principal, Larissa Adam, celebrated with us at the mural installation party and encouraged our continued collaboration and mainstreaming projects.

If you ever take the BART to East 12th Street, look closely and you just might see a rush of red, blue, and pink. The mural serves as a lasting reminder of the power of love, inclusion, and high expectations. These became hallmarks in my approach to both teaching and parenting, and these are also the essential themes that tie this book together.

Introduction

"Did you see Ann's post on Facebook?" my husband Chris asked as I came downstairs after tucking in our daughter.

Ann and I had been close friends in college. However, since graduation, we'd only stayed in touch casually. We followed each other's journeys over social media, celebrating new jobs, the births and adoptions of our kiddos, and each other's birthdays. We hadn't seen each other in years. I picked up my phone and scrolled to her post. It was a call for help.

Ann and her husband were just starting to navigate special education services with their son. She was feeling a huge range of complicated emotions, including worry and isolation. It was a staggeringly honest post that was both smart and courageous, two qualities I'd admired in Ann during those years in college. I reached out.

"Hi, friend." I typed. "Sending love. We've also been through the IEP [Individualized Education Program] process as parents. I'm not sure if you knew, but I worked as a special education teacher for many years. How can I help?"

She responded instantly, and we chatted about her son and the meetings her family was having with specialists. Their son was 3 years old, and they'd been working closely to address his needs since he was an infant.

At one point, I texted her the following:

> Early intervention and therapy are powerful! It is a long road, but this is absolutely the best time to grow. Depending on the services you all are getting, you may have to advocate to get your son everything he needs. And you and your partner know better than anyone else

1

what those needs are. If the IEP team is not making you feel that way, then let's think through how to make sure you are being heard.

I don't know what the early childhood program looks like in your district; however, his school program should help make sure he (and you) feel supported and included. You likely already use social scripts and social stories with him; these can be very helpful in new (and everyday) situations.

Enough on the practical stuff—let's talk personal. Everything you are feeling is valid. It is a hard process. Your son is loved, and you are truly his most important and knowledgeable advocate.

Ann and I talked a little longer about advocacy, social stories, and feelings. We agreed that parenting is hard. I sent her a few heart emojis because sometimes those pink and red shapes offer the best approximation of what you are trying to tell a friend over text. Finally, we said goodnight.

Afterward Chris told me, "You know, Ann's right. There's not enough information out there for parents. You should write a book for families on how to navigate this process."

This is that book.

How to Use This Book

I am assuming (always dangerous) that if you picked up this book, you care for an exceptional child who learns differently. If that is true, I wrote this book specifically for you! If that is not true, something drew you to open these pages and start reading. Maybe you're getting to know a new family in your neighborhood, and they have a child with disabilities. Maybe you're an educator and more children with IEPs keep appearing on your rosters. Maybe you're interested in educational issues or civil rights. Maybe *you* always learned differently and wonder if this book will help you make sense of some of your own experiences in school. Whatever the reason, I encourage you to trust your instincts and keep reading. The more people we can bring to the conversation around inclusion, the better for everyone.

When Your Child Learns Differently can be read cover to cover, in sections, or by individual chapters. In its entirety, it will give you a wealth of knowledge about special education services spanning from early childhood to postsecondary planning. You'll have some ideas of what to expect from the initial referral through your child's last annual IEP. Perhaps you have a specific topic or question that drew you to this text. If so, you might want to start with one of the four parts of this book. Finally, the chapters were written so that they can be read independently to meet your family's immediate needs. The following pages include a Reader's Guide with more information about each chapter, part, and some notes on when this information may be most useful to you.

A Reader's Guide		
Part I: Navigating Services With Hope and Knowledge		
Chapter	**Purpose**	**Read This When . . .**
1	This chapter introduces the big ideas, experiences, and perspectives that have shaped my advice for caring for children who learn differently.	The first chapter is always a good place to start. In this chapter, I share how I learned about special education, both as a teacher and a parent.
2	This chapter provides a foundational guide to important policies and terms to help you navigate the special education and identification processes.	If you are new to special education, starting the evaluation process, or preparing for your initial IEP meeting, this chapter will help you make sense of important terms and policies. The charts are also helpful resources to refer back to as needed.
3	The IEP meeting is an important touchpoint in your child's education. This chapter helps you know what to expect at an IEP meeting and gives you strategies for making your child's IEP more effective.	It can be intimidating to walk into an IEP meeting. Read this chapter to increase your confidence and knowledge before IEP meetings.
Part II: Advocating With Love		
Chapter	**Purpose**	**Read This When . . .**
4	Advocacy is central to both parenting and special education. This chapter gives you tools to use a strengths-based approach to navigate and advocate for your child's unique needs.	There will be times when you will need to intervene on behalf of your child. This chapter will give you language and tools to advocate across a variety of settings to make sure your child is included, receiving the services they need, and treated in ways that are accepting and appropriate.
5	In this chapter, we'll explore the critical positive difference that being "raised on love" makes in child development. We'll also cover tough and important topics ranging from what inclusion looks like in early-elementary classrooms to what life might look like after high school. The central theme of this chapter (and the book, for that matter) is that love is the most important factor in helping children succeed.	In a world with a lot of pressure to be like everyone else, what do school and life look like for children who learn differently? How can we support the social-emotional learning of children with disabilities and create more equitable learning environments? Read this chapter when you are wrestling with these questions or need a reminder about the importance of love in raising children who learn differently.

A Reader's Guide		
Part III: Operationalizing High Expectations		
Chapter	**Purpose**	**Read This When . . .**
6	We don't know what is possible until we try it. This is particularly true when it comes to high expectations for children who learn differently. This chapter explores how to operationalize high expectations with specific extended sections on reading and math.	Are you wondering what high expectations look like for children with disabilities? This chapter offers key considerations for how to nurture ambition and support reading and math development for students who learn differently and at a different pace than their peers.
7	What is exceptionality? What does it mean to learn differently? This chapter celebrates individuals who learn differently and also offers specific information to help children who are navigating multiple identities. Learn more about neurodiversity, representation, disproportionality, and special populations, including twice-exceptional students and English language learners.	Oftentimes the way that disability is framed feels incongruent with the way we see our children. Read this chapter for ideas on reframing disability from a strengths-based perspective. Continue reading for a nuanced discussion of the ways that multiple identities can intersect with ability/disability.
Part IV: Giving Yourself Grace		
Chapter	**Purpose**	**Read This When . . .**
8	All of the feelings and experiences you have while raising a child who learns differently are valid. This chapter, told with both candor and optimism, offers a frank discussion about navigating the great adventures of parenting exceptional children while also taking care of yourself.	Read and revisit this chapter whenever you could use a little extra support or a reminder that you are not alone. In fact, if this is the reminder you most needed when you picked up this book, read this chapter first, then start at the beginning, and work your way back again.

Part I

Navigating Services With Hope and Knowledge

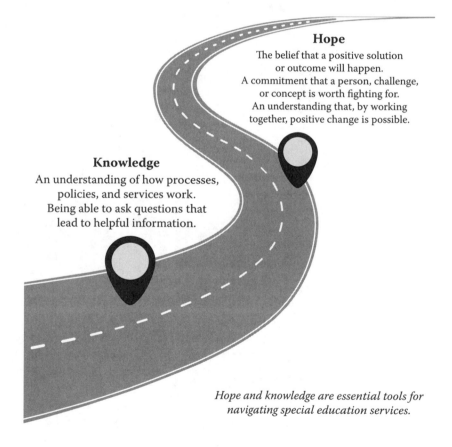

Hope
The belief that a positive solution
or outcome will happen.
A commitment that a person, challenge,
or concept is worth fighting for.
An understanding that, by working
together, positive change is possible.

Knowledge
An understanding of how processes,
policies, and services work.
Being able to ask questions that
lead to helpful information.

*Hope and knowledge are essential tools for
navigating special education services.*

Chapter 1

Caring for Kids Who Learn Differently

In a world with a lot of pressure to be "normal," this book celebrates exceptionality. To be *exceptional* means to differ from the norm. Although there are many ways to be different, this book affirms our children who learn differently. When we listen to children who learn differently, we all benefit from seeing the world, ideas, and relationships in ways we could have never imagined. Exceptionality isn't easy, and it certainly doesn't always feel beautiful. For children and families alike, learning differently often feels like temper tantrums, hurt feelings, and dead ends.

"Wait!" I can hear you saying. "I thought this was an inspirational book about love and high expectations."

It is. I believe honesty is the most helpful form of inspiration. We all need a friend who tells it to us straight. I am going to do my best to practice courage and be that person for you. Over the next several chapters, I'll share candidly what I've learned about parenting and caring for children who experience school (and life) differently than their peers.

I am hoping that, in sharing stories of exceptional children I've known and cared for, I can help reframe the way we think about difference. Parenting is hard work. Sometimes we all need a friend. This book is my invitation for us to talk honestly, as friends, about *our* kids. I can imagine this conversation over a mug of hot tea, a long walk, or a big piece of chocolate cake.

Although my experiences are not exactly the same as yours, we can all learn from each other's stories. The following chapters offer information about support plans, policy, research, and plenty of colorful anecdotes from my personal and professional life working with and caring for children who learn differently. Navigating the world of special education services, creating individualized support plans, and advocating for your child's needs are big and important tasks. Advocacy requires courage, strength, and often leaps of faith. Just as there are infinite ways to be different, there are also infinite ways to support and advocate for children. We'll talk about this as we honor the different and multiple exceptionalities our children have. Many of the books I've read on advocating for children with disabilities presuppose an adversarial relationship between families and schools. I want to offer another approach.

I wrote this book to give you specific and practical tools. Entering the world of special education services can feel like learning a new language; it's a bit like swimming through the policy waters of acronym soup. Often families don't learn these particulars until they're suddenly immersed in them. I want to help ease that learning curve and give you the confidence you need to be the most effective and most important advocate in your child's life.

Along the way, it's easy to feel all alone. You are not alone. There is a vast community of families who care for children who learn differently, who need extra support in schools, and/or who have disabilities. Sometimes you need specific information about legislation, jargon, organizations, and procedures. Sometimes you need to hear from another parent who has been through something similar. Sometimes you need all of this, and also a hug.

Please feel free to share this book with others in your family community. Bring it along to IEP meetings and share it with your partner, with grandparents, and even with your child's teachers. Although there are lots of books out there for educators, I found that there weren't enough written for families. My personal experiences as both a special education teacher and a parent to a child with an IEP inform the guidance, stories, and information I offer throughout these pages.

My husband and I recently celebrated our son's graduation from high school—and, friends, it doesn't get easier. Well, some things get easier, and other things get harder. Does this pattern that begins with worrying and ends with your child finding their way sound familiar? You worry when your child starts a new school, service, or class. You fret. You don't know if you made the right choice, and then, to your surprise, it starts off fine. One success leads to another. You breathe a sigh of relief—and then suddenly there's a big setback. It shakes you to your core and seems to validate all of your concerns. Before you can recover, there's another setback. Slowly you overcome that challenge together, and then you get past the next challenge. With this success, you breathe a more cautious sigh of hope.

This process repeats a million times throughout every school year. Then, one day you step back and notice that your children are starting to find their way. When does that day come, and how long does it last? I don't know yet; I am still figuring this out, and everyone's experience is different. What I do know is that, despite all of our planning and personal ideas about when someone should learn certain skills, our children will navigate life on their own terms and at their own pace. My oldest child is grown, and we are still learning this—every day. The advocacy, navigating, worrying, loving, celebrating, and support planning never end.

Looking back at those elementary, middle school, and high school years, what advice would I give to families starting this journey? What do I wish my family had known? What would I do differently if I had it to do again? Over the next several chapters, we'll explore these questions together over a proverbial cup of tea. This is a book about navigating special education services from the inside out and outside in. This is also a book about finding our way and thinking together about how to support the children we love and the vision we share for inclusion.

Different Ways to Be Different

A few minutes before the graduation ceremony, Kaci called me over: "Dr. Fishman-Weaver, you know how we all have to move our tassels from right to left at the end of the ceremony?"

I paused, embarrassed that I missed checking in with her about this earlier. Kaci uses a power chair and has limited mobility. I hadn't thought about the complications of this graduation tradition until just this moment.

"Oh, yes. Do you want me to find you a friend?" I asked.

"Nope. I'm good. Watch." She blinked her eyes dramatically, smiled, and twirled her head as if playing with a hula hoop. Her tassel glided gracefully from the right to left.

We both laughed out loud. This is *so Kaci*.

Kaci was a top student in her graduating class and the president of our honor society. She lit up the room with her smile, positive attitude, and sense of humor. In fact, just hearing her name at faculty meetings made everyone smile. Kaci practices self-advocacy with a warmth and humor to which we should all aspire.

In this brief vignette are themes of love, humor, and high expectations. These themes are threads throughout this book. Disability and difference are complex. Even as I demystify lots of processes, policies, practices, and acronyms, I have no intention of simplifying *identity*. Our children are layered and multifaceted. Our children are leading story-rich journeys, and it is our privilege to celebrate and join them on these adventures.

Many wonderful things happened when I started writing this book. My favorite was how people started coming up to me to share stories about children they love who learn differently. These stories were joyful, courageous, difficult, and real:

> ›   "Yesterday was our son's IEP, and something strange happened when we were talking about his goals. . . ."
> ›   "Last night, my daughter and I were talking, and she said something that broke my heart. . . ."
> ›   "Can I tell you about the brave choice my daughter made yesterday?"
> ›   "His teachers just don't understand what anxiety means for my son. . . ."
> ›   "What happens after high school?"

In many ways, these stories shaped the narrative arc of the following chapters. I am grateful that there was so much interest in this project early on; this interest both encouraged me and guided the scope of this project. As people offered stories of their children, I listened for points of connection. Although the stories were different, many of the concerns were the same. The more I visited with families who identified as having children who learn or experience school differently, the more certain types of questions kept coming up:

> ›   "How can we support children who experience school differently from their peers?"
> ›   "What supports and services are available to help my child, and how can we access them?"
> ›   "What do you mean when you say to advocate with love and high expectations?"
> ›   "Why do I feel so alone?"
> ›   "What are our educational rights?"
> ›   "Why don't teachers understand my child?"

Sometimes families heard about this project and asked me if this book was for them. They said things like:

> "My child doesn't receive services, but he does learn differently."
> "My child does receive services, but I don't think of her as a special education student."
> "I am raising my grandson. Does your book talk about the role of grandparents?"
> "We've never had her tested, but something is going on."

These comments and questions are important, and my hope is that, yes, this book is for all of you. I hope this book gives you guidance, affirmation, and friendship. I also hope to normalize some of the big feelings that often come with loving children who learn differently. There are many ways to learn differently or to be different. I know that each of our children are uniquely nuanced, idiosyncratic, and special in their own ways.

Visible and Invisible Disabilities

Students with learning differences or disabilities often face biases and misperceptions about their talents, capabilities, and complexities. This is true whether students have invisible or visible disabilities. *Invisible disabilities* refer to disabilities that are not obvious to an onlooker (e.g., dyslexia, learning disabilities, etc.). *Visible disabilities* refer to disabilities that may be obvious to an onlooker (e.g., orthopedic impairment, Down syndrome, etc.). Often the challenges of individuals with invisible disabilities are misunderstood by everyone, from the general public to your child's classroom teacher ("Why is your child behaving that way?"), whereas the challenges of individuals with visible disabilities are overexaggerated by the general public ("Oh, I assumed your child couldn't do that.").

Despite these misperceptions, almost everyone is personally connected to someone with a disability. We have colleagues, family members, children, peers, and friends who have disabilities. Many of us also have personal disabilities. Depending on how they are defined, somewhere between 10%–20% of the population have disabilities. The U.S. Census Bureau (2012) reported that close to 19% of the population self-identified as having a disability (broadly defined) in 2010. Nearly half of those people said that their disability was severe. Many of these disabilities are not obvious to strangers. A 1994 study (Invisible Disabilities Association, n.d.) indicated that 75% of individuals with disabilities have invisible disabilities.

Having a disability in one area does not mean having a disability in another area. Kaci, for example, has both specific medical needs and strong academic skills. Although she sometimes experienced school differently than her peers, she also excelled in challenging classes, made friends, and was a leader to her peers. She has continued to take on important leadership roles in college. I've had the opportunity to work with many exceptional students like Kaci who have taught me again and again that people are not "either/or"; instead, we are all "both/and."

In fact, students with disabilities often have *asynchronous development*, which refers to skills that develop at different rates and paces from each other. For example, a middle school child may be a gifted mathematician and struggle with interpersonal peer relationships; an elementary student may not yet be able to have a simple conversation, but can draw complex and realistic landscapes. For more information on asynchronous development, see the discussion on twice-exceptional students (pp. 139–142). Honoring the unique ways our children shine, giving them grace and support for the areas in which they are developing, and being unwavering in our belief that all children are capable of great things are three of the most important lessons I've learned in caring for children who learn differently.

Becoming a Special Education Teacher

I often say I fell sideways into teaching. Here's the story. I was working my first "real job" as an in-house publicist for a social justice nonprofit. The plan was to keep this position for a couple years and then study public health at the University of California, Berkeley. My plans changed. The romantic version of my story is that I was taking the BART home from work and saw an advertisement about the dire need for special education teachers in Oakland's public schools. Like most romantic versions of stories, this is true—and oversimplified.

The story really starts several years earlier when a family member had to spend some time at a children's hospital. This meant that I also spent a lot of time at the children's hospital. While there, I observed the hospital special education teacher. I never talked to her, but I witnessed the magic that surrounded her work[2]. Here were young people going through bigger challenges than I could ever imagine. Yet, when I peered into their rooms while they were with the teacher, they were giggling over fiction books, puzzling over math problems, and even conducting science experiments. For those few moments they were just kids. As I watched this teacher, I began to think that maybe special education is a public health job. Several years later, it turned out that it was, in fact, just the public health profession for me.

During college, I volunteered through our service learning department. I always chose service options with students. I served as a tutor for students at our Centro Latino, as a teacher assistant in a special education classroom, and as a coach at a therapeutic riding center for students (and adults) with disabilities. All of these experiences flashed through my memory like a movie as I read that announcement on the BART. The stars aligned, and I knew what I wanted to do next. When I arrived home, I told Chris that I was going to apply for a position in special education. He was stir-frying vegetables for dinner. I slid in next to him to wash my hands and chop bell peppers. We were living in a studio apartment in Berkeley, which meant that by proximity alone, all of our conversations felt intimate and deep.

"Special education?" he asked, and I nodded. "That sounds great, honey."

Filtering Difference

As a student teacher, I was placed in a preschool classroom for 3- and 4-year-old children with autism. We sang songs at morning meeting, colored pictures, read books, and giggled at the wonders of the world. Each of my students was approximately 30 pounds of joy, innocence, and quirky personality. I didn't yet have children of my own, and neither did Matthew, my colleague who also was assigned to student teach in the same class. On the rare occasions when Matthew or I interacted with young children outside of our classroom, we were often surprised by their communication skills.

We had both been hired on an emergency credential, which meant that our preteaching coursework was greatly accelerated. We did our most

---

2 Twenty years later I met this teacher again and got to tell her what an inspiration she had been to me!

important learning on the job and took graduate courses in education in the evenings. We didn't yet have a frame of reference to understand (or notice) our students' differences. We didn't think of our sweet preschoolers as *different*; to us, they were just children. Part of this was due to a lack of experience with young children, but mostly it had to do with the fact that we knew these young children simply as kids—kids we cared about.

Now I do have children of my own and multiple degrees in education, but there's something about this filter that has stayed with me. We don't see difference in the same way when we start with love. The classroom where I student taught was for students with moderate to severe needs. Most of our children used gesture to communicate or were still in the echolalic[3] stage. Many outsiders (or professionals) would have considered our students very different from the norm. To us, though, they were simply (and wonderfully) our students.

Of course, you know and love your child's unique and quirky personality. Yes, you sometimes have to explain to teachers that your daughter needs certain routines to be successful at school. At the end of the day though, you see your kid as a kid first, second, and third. You see how she lights up when her favorite song comes on. You know how to draw circles on his back if he is scared to help him calm down. You have your child's favorite books memorized, and you can pick her laugh out of a crowd. Over the next several chapters we'll talk a lot about what difference and disability do and don't tell us, and we'll explore how love and naivety are often important gifts in working with children.

My First Classroom

When I started teaching, the urban district I served had just regained local control of the public schools from state intervention. As a result of the transition, the district was experiencing what some called a "small schools revolution." Smaller schools were being created on two fronts: Bigger schools were being divided into smaller schools, and small neighborhood schools were being built. The school where I learned to be a teacher was one of these new neighborhood schools. Parents of the neighborhood had rallied for a school for their children, which resulted in the bright blue and orange K–8 building that I came to love.

---

3 Repeated speech as a child learns to speak.

However, when the original architectural plans were drawn, no one had considered classrooms or services for students with disabilities. In 2006, when I started teaching, the district changed requirements so that all public schools had to offer programming for students with disabilities. Enter 24-year-old me and a group of students who reframed everything I thought I knew about teaching, learning, and ability.

Our principal worked with me to find a space for my first- to third-grade students. This was the first self-contained class in our building. My very young students and I shared space in the eighth-grade wing. My students were also the only students who didn't live in the neighborhood. In fact, almost all of them were bussed in. Further, my class represented the largest proportion of African American students in our school. Ninety percent of our school population were neighborhood kids whose home language was Spanish, many of whom had recently immigrated from Central or South America. As a White woman in her twenties, I spoke broken Spanish and had big dreams about the world. As it turns out, we were all trying to find our way in the complex political and personal landscape.

Many people in our community were apprehensive about my student population. The task of starting up all of these special education programs was a huge undertaking for an underresourced urban district. There was a lot of learning that happened in our district, in our school, and for me during that first year teaching. On my very first day of school, bus routes were not yet worked out, and I only had one student arrive. Luiza's mother dropped off one of the kindest and gentlest human beings I've ever known. A tiny girl, who kept her long dark hair in a neat ponytail, Luiza immediately took my hand, beamed up at me and said, "Hola, maestra."[4]

We walked hand-in-hand back to the classroom. We read books, giggled, and painted pictures. She told me simple stories about her paintings: "This is a flower. This is a tree. This is my mama." And so on. I noticed that in one of the pictures she had painted a pink "v" in what looked like a bright blue sky. I asked her to tell me about it.

She smiled. "That is an angel to look over our classroom."

I tacked that painting above our classroom door, and true to her word, Luiza's angel watched over us every day for the 3 years that my program ran.

---

4 Spanish for: Hello, teacher.

A Community Approach

A month or so into that first school year, Ms. Tonnesha Pace (a parent at our school) joined our classroom community as a paraprofessional. Together we set routines, worked with small groups, and loved our students. Ms. Pace knew the community. Her daughter attended the school. She had watched the first few weeks as our class tried to integrate into the school. She was there the day our first paraprofessional ran (literally) away. Our principal and others had told her, "You know kids. You're a mom. You should join their community." They might have also said, "You should go help that new teacher out." And blessing upon blessing, she did. As a mother, nothing fazed her. She saw when kids needed tissues or a hug or a firm, warm voice. Love and high expectations were how she ran her home, and this classroom quickly became an extension of both our homes.

In addition to Ms. Pace, I had Gah-mel's auntie, Demarco's grandma, Christian's mom, and Isaac's grandma to see me through. These women sat with me before or after school while their children sprawled on the bright-colored carpet and built structures out of LEGO bricks. Sometimes they brought still-warm tamales, hot coffee, or, if I was really lucky, a piece of sweet potato pie to share.

In an article for *Principal Leadership*, I wrote (Fishman-Weaver, 2018a),

> I wouldn't have survived that first year, were it not for my students' grandmothers and aunties who mentored me, the night custodian who visited with me when we were the only ones left in the building, the cafeteria worker who helped me send food home to hungry students, and the secretary who translated my notes from English to Spanish. These first few years working at that school taught me some of the most important lessons I've learned about education and community. (para. 7)

I believe school, just like raising children, is a community project. I share these reflections to remind you that we are *all* figuring it out together. Love and high expectations work best in communities. Visit with your child's classroom teachers, sit together, volunteer in the room, and share stories about the young person you both care for. Also, it never hurts to remember that we could all use another cup of coffee.

High Expectations: A Self-Fulfilling Prophecy

Another product of the scattered nature of beginning so many special education programs across the district was that my students' IEPs took almost two months to arrive. (For lots of information on IEPs, see Chapter 3.) This delay turned out to be a blessing. Although IEPs give us important information, kids give us the most important information. By the time these documents finally arrived, many of the passages didn't sound like the children I'd already come to care for. I read accounts of how my students "would never learn to communicate properly," "would always struggle with reading," and "were unlikely to learn how to write." I looked around our sunny classroom at students who were engaged in board games, chatting over picture books, and learning to write topic sentences and poems.

This is when I learned about the self-fulfilling prophecy of high expectations. I fervently believed that all of the children in my classroom could and would learn how to read, write, solve math problems, and make friends. I believed that, with enough opportunities for learning and with enough support and love, we'd all get there. And we did.

Even as our students were learning these things, our classroom wasn't without its challenges. Early in the school year, the teacher next door came into my room at the end of the day (peak transition time), and she was shocked. Some students were crying, others were running, and suddenly a backpack flew through the air. I looked at my colleague and watched as the color drained from her face. We had countless moments of chaos. Children, classrooms, parents, and communities are all "both/and." My classroom was *both* rewarding, fulfilling, celebratory, *and* challenging, confusing, and frustrating. Pulling back the proverbial curtain to share this range of experiences leads to more honest dialogue about the complicated nature of raising children. I believe everyone would benefit from more honesty about the joys and challenges that come from parenting and teaching children who learn differently.

After 3 years, the district decided to recentralize special education services by moving self-contained classrooms like mine back out of our small neighborhood schools and into fewer bigger schools. At this point, all of my students were reading and writing at varying levels. Our class was the first special education class in the district to adopt the new general education rigorous mathematics program, and my students had risen to the occasion. One-hundred percent of my students were mainstreamed in general education classes. We had self-published two books, performed in assemblies, and helped create two educational murals, including the one featured on the cover of this book. Several of my students were moving out of my special education class and into general education classes with some support, and two had exited special education services altogether. (For more information about the continuum of services see p. 80.)

As I started writing this book, the first graders mentioned in this section were celebrating their high school graduations. With high expectations and lots of opportunities for learning, practice, and abundant support, children are capable of amazing things.

Becoming a Mother

Jaxon, a student in my first group of first-grade students, was a confident African American boy with more charisma than he knew what to do with. He was even smaller than Luiza. He had a huge smile that charmed the toughest of adults. He shook visitors' hands like a grown-up and looked them in the eye with a poise that took people by surprise. He was the strongest reader in my class and absolutely couldn't sit still. A talented athlete, Jaxon frequently kicked soccer balls over the 12-foot barbed-wire fences that lined our school property.

One day we were outside at recess, and he asked if we could talk. We ducked into a nearby kindergarten classroom and sat together on miniature red and yellow plastic chairs.

He looked at me and asked, "Would you be my mom?"

Time stopped.

Over the years, other students would ask me this, in a sort of sweet jest. For example, Ana's mom told me about a regular drama that occurred at their house. She would ask Ana to brush her teeth. Ana would storm off, stuff her pajamas in a grocery bag, and say, "I am going to my teacher's. She loves me and won't make me do things like that." *Au contraire*, my dear.

Jaxon's request was not in jest. Jaxon was one of 400,000 children in the United States foster care system. Of these children, more than 100,000 are waiting to be adopted (AdoptUSKids, n.d.). My husband and I knew virtually nothing about the foster adoption process. Not knowing all of the details or processes and still jumping in for children is a common narrative in this book. So is what we did next. We connected with as many people who could help us as possible. We found a kind social worker, another adoptive dad, a brilliant public defender, and a retired principal—all were willing to hold our hands figuratively and literally.

So much of parenting is about saying yes to challenges we're not sure how to tackle. We reach out for any supports we can find—books, friends, blog posts, our own parents—and although we don't know what we're doing, we commit to figuring it out together. Over and over again, we use faith and love to find our way.

Then, in the evening we turn to our partner and say, "Are we going to be okay? Yes, I think we're going to be okay."

This is often followed by, "Whew, I need to [take a walk, have a drink, call my mom]."

Chris and I had never considered adoption. To be honest, we hadn't even really considered parenting. We fell in love young and were married just out of college. It turns out, with parenting, you don't always get to pick your adventures; usually they're just given to you. This is true however you grow your family.

Chris and I were both at work the day we got the call that we could pick up our son forever. We rushed over in separate cars. Jaxon looked so small climbing into my car. I drove with one eye on the road and the other on the mirror watching this tiny child who was now my son. Jaxon knew me as "Mrs. K," a teacher at his school. I told him I wasn't going to be Mrs. K to him anymore. I asked if he knew what to call me.

A smile grew across his face; it is a smile I will never forget. "Does it start with an 'm'?" he asked, his eyes dancing with hope.

We've been Mom and Dad ever since.

That night we went out to a pizza parlor to celebrate. Jaxon asked if he could play a pinball game. Before we could answer, he'd already jumped up and ran across the restaurant.

"Do we let him go by himself?" my husband asked.

"I think . . . it's okay," I said, not 100% sure.

Like all new parents, we were terrified, naive, and hadn't known that our hearts could stretch so big. Jaxon joined our family when he was 8 years old. His adoption was finalized 2 years later when a judge made legal what we'd known in our hearts for years—that we belong together.

Along the way, many people asked if we "knew what we were getting into." Of course we didn't. With parenting, you never know what you are getting into. Several people talked to us about Jaxon's disabilities. Some of them were right in their assessments, and many were wrong. Too many people talked to us only about race, and not enough people talked to us about the long-lasting social-emotional effects of foster care.

We brushed aside all of the concerning comments and told everyone we were "sure it would all be fine; after all, love is the most important thing."

The year the adoption was finalized was the same year that our school district decided to recentralize special education services. This seemed like the right moment for us to move back to the Midwest so our son could grow up closer to his grandparents. Doing so also started me on a new adventure working with high school students.

Whether They're 7 or 17

I returned to the high school that I had graduated from and was the given the opportunity to teach math, finance, and reading to high school students with disabilities. I used the same philosophy that had worked in my elementary classroom. I believed that:

> ›   students will meet the expectations we set for them, and
> ›   setting high expectations—and supporting students in reaching those expectations—is an act of love.

For the most part, this philosophy proved as effective in the high school as it had in my elementary classrooms. My students and I orchestrated projects and met standards that were considered "impossible" for our self-contained math and finance classes. My finance students self-published a book on understanding financial institutions that was covered by our local newspaper and gave the general education finance teacher new ideas about how to restructure his class. At the end of the year, several of the students in my self-contained math class were able to join their general education peers in the regular algebra track.

I promised that I would tell it you straight, so I want to be perfectly clear that my high school classes weren't all sunshine and success stories. There was a lot of work, heartache, insecurity, more than a few curse words, several textbooks thrown across the classroom, lots of eye rolling, and some tears along the way. Although we did experience tremendous success, there were always a few students who didn't make the progress I wanted. Travis was one of these students.

Travis made everybody laugh, including his teachers, even when they were frustrated with him. Athletic, well-dressed, and constantly in trouble (big and small), Travis was regularly late for class. His schoolwork was perpetually missing, late, or incomplete. He had yet to master the art of thinking before speaking. During his junior year, he was several credits behind and enrolled in three of my classes. Two were academic classes, and the third was a resource class in which Travis was supposed to work on his homework and organize his studies to get back on track for graduation. I had his mother on speed dial. She was doing the best she could but also at her wits' end. After his junior year, I rarely saw Travis. When I inquired about him with other students and even teachers, I heard stories. I wasn't completely sure if they were rumors, exaggeration, or the truth. I hoped they weren't true. Eventually, Travis did graduate high school, and although I thought of him, as I expected, we didn't stay in touch.

Five years later, Travis shocked us when he came back to visit several teachers at school. He was now a young man and told us he was taking community college classes, working as a first responder, and in a serious relationship. He said he was sorry for all of the trouble he had caused and that he had just come back to say thank you. Caring for kids who learn differently is about the long game. Sometimes that game is very long. Often there are detours, tears, and even crises along the way.

I share Travis's story to illustrate how a kid with a whole lot of potential—who, yes, got into trouble—eventually found his way. I bet many folks reading this book can see themselves in Travis's mom, who always answered the phone when I called, who said with tired heaviness in her voice that, yes, she would talk with Travis about his homework, his attitude, or that office referral when he got home. If she found any schoolwork lying around the house, she would bring it to school in case it was missing homework. She wasn't always as patient as she wanted to be, and she certainly wasn't always optimistic, but she loved her son. She saw him at his best and at his worst, and kept showing up for him. I believe this made all of the difference, even as there were some very hard years along the way.

It was my privilege to be a small part of Travis's life for a short of period time. It was also a gift I'll never forget that he came back to share that he was indeed finding his way. My students have taught me that each of us takes our own path to success. In my career in education, I've been inspired by children who have overcome significant challenges, kids who have persevered, and kids who have taught me to see the world differently. Sometimes the road ahead looks treacherous. Sometimes the obstacles feel insurmountable. When this happens, know that, with patience, courage, love, and high expectations, you and your child can navigate just about any challenge. Young people are infinitely more resilient and resourceful than adults. Caring for kids who learn differently is about honoring that resilience, encouraging resourcefulness, patiently advocating, and never giving up on nurturing ambition. Knowing that family advocacy is both an art and a skill, in the next chapter, I'll answer some language and process questions you may be having as you start this journey into special education services and supports.

Chapter 2

Understanding Special Education Policy

I once told a friend that special education policy could best be summarized by the statement, "All children are entitled to FAPE in the LRE." She raised her left eyebrow and looked at me as though I were speaking in another language. She wasn't wrong. Navigating special education services can feel like you are learning a new language. There are so many policies, procedures, and acronyms. Most of these are unfamiliar unless you have been through the special education process before. This chapter gives you a broad overview of special education policy, with particular attention to important terms and concepts you will likely encounter, from the identification of a disability through your last annual IEP meeting. By the end of this chapter, if I tell you, "All children are entitled to FAPE in the LRE," my hope is that you will nod and say, "Of course they are."

Policy History: How Parent Advocates Made Special Education History

My maternal grandmother taught in a one-room schoolhouse in the late 1940s. One year, a student with profound disabilities joined her class. My grandmother said she went home that night and cried herself to sleep.

While reliving the memory, she said, "Honey, I had no idea how to teach her."

My grandmother did what we all do in that situation—the best she knew how. She made sure the student was included, safe, and learning. This happens to be the same advice I'd give to anyone who is uncertain of how to support a child who learns differently. At the time when my grandmother was teaching in that little red schoolhouse, there weren't policies and research-based best practices to point her to, so she had to use love and what she knew about K–8 learning to find her way through.

After that year, my grandmother left teaching to raise her family and support my grandfather in running our family farm. My grandmother is 90 years old now. She and that student still live in the same small country town in Iowa, and occasionally they run into each other at the grocery store. Every time they see each other, the woman comes up to my grandmother, hugs her, and says, "Oh, I know you. You were my teacher!"

Relationships are the heart of education, learning, and advocacy. The special education policy story began outside of schools, organized by concerned parents and supported by social, political, and religious leaders. Together, they paved the way for our commitment to educate *all* students through public education. This commitment sets the U.S. apart from many countries. When I speak about our educational system internationally, this commitment is one of my greatest sources of pride about our public schools. Remember, achieving this inclusive philosophy is fairly recent in legislative history. Further, like all civil rights decisions, it requires the continued advocacy of parents, teachers, educational leaders, and students.

In the 1950s and 1960s, the Civil Rights Movement provided a rich climate to expand access and inclusion for many marginalized groups, including children with disabilities. The *Brown v. Board of Education* decision of 1954, which ruled that it was unconstitutional for schools to segregate based on race, set the stage for other groups to explore the negative impacts of segregation in schools and to fight for greater inclusion. Prior to the legislative victories outlined in the following paragraphs, children with moderate to profound disabilities were often excluded from public schools and told that they could only receive services at institutions for the "mentally handicapped." Their parents either kept these children at home or had to send them away.

Research shows what parents already knew: that segregating students is psychologically damaging (Wineburg, 1987). Separating children on the basis of identity (e.g., skin color, disability, etc.) is unhealthy and runs counter to the democratic ideals of public education in the U.S. Family advocacy groups fought for better practices to educate their children with disabilities—and they won! In 1965, the Elementary and Secondary Education Act and the Public Law 89-313 program provided states with direct grant assistance to help educate children with disabilities. These acts were followed by the Handicapped Children's Early Education Assistance Act of 1968 and the Economic Opportunities Amendments of 1972.

Yet, even with these provisions, in 1970 U.S. schools were still only educating one in five children with disabilities. Many states still had laws excluding certain students from school, including children who were deaf, blind, emotionally disturbed, or cognitively impaired (U.S. Department of Education, 2008). And so, families and support groups started taking legislative action. Key court cases, including *Pennsylvania Association for Retarded Citizens v. Commonwealth* (1971) and *Mills v. Board of Education of the District of Columbia* (1972), created a legal precedent for protecting and advocating for the rights of people with disabilities.

On November 29, 1975, President Gerald Ford signed into law the Education for All Handicapped Children Act. According to the Office of Special Education and Rehabilitative Services (2010),

> In adopting this landmark civil rights measure, Congress opened public school doors for millions of children with disabilities and laid the foundation of the country's commitment to ensuring that children with disabilities have opportunities to develop their talents, share their gifts, and contribute to their communities. (para. 2)

In 1990, the Education for All Handicapped Children Act was reauthorized as the Individuals with Disabilities Education Act (IDEA). With the authorization of IDEA, every student was now guaranteed access to a free, appropriate, public education (FAPE) in the least restrictive environment (LRE). These terms are further defined in following section. In 2004, IDEA was reauthorized again as the Individuals with Disabilities Education Improvement Act to include more provisions for early intervention and disproportionality.

A Guide to Acronym Soup

Special education is full of jargon and acronyms (see Figure 1). Let's untangle some of the terms you will encounter while working on support

A Family Guide to Acronyms in Special Education

Acronym	Term	Notes and Family Impact
ADA	Americans with Disabilities Act	This civil rights law prohibits discrimination against individuals with disabilities in all areas of public life, including school. The ADA protects the rights of people with disabilities (including children), ensuring that they have the same rights and opportunities as everyone else. The ADA was signed into law in 1990.
AT	Assistive technology	This refers to the equipment, technology, or products (hardware or software) that support the functioning, and often communication needs, of students with disabilities. AT is included in potential resources for students with disabilities under IDEA.
DOE	U.S. Department of Education	Students with disabilities are protected by federal legislation, including IDEA. States (and schools) have latitude to do more than is outlined by the DOE and this legislation, but not less.
FAPE	Free and appropriate public education	Under IDEA, all students are entitled to be included in the public education system and to be educated in classrooms and programs that fit their needs, at no cost to the family.
IDEA	Individuals with Disabilities Education Act	This is the federal law governing special education. (*Note.* IDEA lists parents first on its list of required members for an IEP team.)
IEP	Individualized Education Program (or Plan)	This legally binding document outlines a student's goals, services, accommodations, and needs, which must be carried out by the public school a child attends. This plan is reviewed annually and may be adapted as needs change. Until a child reaches the age of majority, a parent or guardian must agree to the evaluations and services in this plan.

Figure 1. Quick guide to 12 common acronyms. *Note.* The acronyms on this chart are pronounced by reading their letters (e.g., I-D-E-A) except for FAPE and SPED, which are pronounced like words.

A Family Guide to Acronyms in Special Education

Acronym	Term	Notes and Family Impact
LEA	Local education agency	The LEA (usually a school administrator or counselor) is the person who guarantees that the school/district can and will provide the accommodations, modifications, and supports agreed to in the IEP. Therefore, an LEA must be present at every IEP meeting.
LRE	Least restrictive environment	LRE, which is a part of IDEA, states that students with disabilities must receive their education, to the maximum extent possible, with their general education or nondisabled peers.
OT	Occupational therapy	This is a related service that might be offered to your child if their fine motor, visual motor, sensory motor, or self-care skills negatively impact school performance. School-based OT does not replace medical OT if needed.
PT	Physical therapy	This related service might be offered to your child if they have functional limitations due to a physical disability or other health-related conditions that limit their ability to access the school environment. School-based PT does not replace medical PT if needed.
SLP	Speech-language pathologist	The SLP may offer related services in speech and language to your child, such as production of sounds, executive functioning, written expression, reading comprehension, abstract reasoning, and social language. With very young children, an SLP may work on feeding and swallowing.
SPED	Special education	SPED is an umbrella term for the cluster of services, programs, and resources to support the needs of students who learn differently.

Figure 1. Continued.

plans and services for your child. Many of these terms are outlined in IDEA. As we review these, I'll share not only what each acronym means, but also how it impacts families. Policy knowledge is important cultural capital in being able to advocate for your exceptional child. That doesn't mean you have to memorize Figure 1. You might bring this chart with you to IEP meetings, refer to it when looking over documents, and add your own notes about how these different acronyms impact your child's educational plan.

Although it is helpful to be as informed as possible, no one expects you to walk into a meeting knowing all of these terms. If you are unfamiliar with a term, policy, or acronym, or if you are unclear on how anything being said applies to your child, pause the meeting and ask for clarification. If I were to summarize this chart to a parent, I would say: *Your child has the right to pursue the best educational path our schools can make available, and you are the most important decision maker in that educational plan.* You don't have to take my word for it; over the next several chapters, I'll share numerous procedures and safeguards that protect this claim.

Disability and Ability

Disability may be one part of your child's identity. Like all identities, there are times when disability feels foregrounded and times when it is less central. What does disability tell us? What *doesn't* disability tell us?

Disability doesn't tell us anything about a child's likes, preferences, strengths, sense of humor, or sense of justice. It doesn't tell us what kind of friend they are to others. It doesn't tell us about your child's smile, charisma, honesty, or perseverance. And—this is very important—it doesn't tell us what young people are capable of. It doesn't tell us what kinds of classes they will take in high school, what their postsecondary journeys will look like, or what kind of adults they will become. In fact, new research in neurodiversity suggests that individuals with disabilities are frequently *more* capable when it comes to certain skills (Armstrong, 2015; Iuculano et al., 2014). For more information on neurodiversity, see Chapter 7.

Okay, so what is a disability? It is largely contextualized by the personal—and social—meanings that individuals ascribe to this identity. This means that families, teachers, and people with disabilities all have a lot of power to reconstruct how we understand disability. As one part of a child's identity, disability can contribute to specific strengths and challenges.

Having a disability is both complex and limited in what it can (and can't) tell us. Further, disability is malleable; how it presents, the meanings we ascribe to it, and the significance it carries can all change over the course of an individual's life.

In terms of policy, the two most important legislative definitions of disabilities come from the ADA and IDEA. These definitions of disability inform many of the services our children will receive in school and beyond. The ADA defines an individual with a disability as "a person who has a physical or mental impairment that substantially limits one or more major life activity" (ADA National Network, 2019). According to the ADA, it is unlawful to discriminate against a person based on ability or disability status. We will revisit the ADA's definition of disability when we explore Section 504 at the end of this chapter.

IDEA defines disability more specifically. In fact, it outlines 13 categories of disabilities (UnderstandingSpecialEducation.com, 2016). Students who are identified as having one of these 13 disabilities may qualify for special education services. The 13 disability categories covered by IDEA include autism, blindness, deafness, emotional disturbance, hearing impairment, intellectual disability, multiple disabilities, orthopedic impairment, other health impairment, specific learning disability, speech or language impairment, traumatic brain injury, and visual impairment.

The U.S. Department of Education (n.d.) reported that there are more than 6.5 million eligible infants, toddlers, children, and youth who receive special education services because of disabilities. This means that if your child is identified as having a disability, you are not alone. The presence of a disability tells us a bit about the kinds of supports, accommodations, or modifications a student is likely to need in school, which can help with support planning. Before we go there, let's talk a little bit about what the identification process looks like.

Determining Eligibility: Initial Identification

Typically, students with medical or more profound disabilities are identified by a doctor very early, well before school age. These students often begin receiving services earlier, are referred for preschool and early-intervention programs, and may have a more streamlined approach to identification for special education. Although medical diagnoses give us important information, a medical diagnosis does not automatically identify a student as having a disability under IDEA. This can be confusing. A medical doctor may diagnosis your child with autism, yet the school will still need to complete an educational evaluation to be sure that (1) your child reaches the criteria under IDEA, and (2) your child needs special education services in school.

Students with mild to moderate disabilities, including specific learning disabilities, are often not identified until they are already in school, sometimes even into middle school. The path to identification for these students is bit more complex and varied. That said, there aren't any hard-and-fast rules here; sometimes students with mild disabilities are identified very young, and likewise, sometimes students with more profound disabilities go undiagnosed or unidentified until later in their school careers. Giftedness can also lead to a late diagnosis or even a misdiagnosis. In Chapter 7, we will briefly explore some of the complexities of twice-exceptional (2e) students, who are both gifted and have a disability. Further, many aspects of ability/disability shift and change over the course of a student's school career. These changes are often noticed by parents and teachers, requiring a revision and sometimes a reevaluation of the child's services, supports, and goals.

If a disability is suspected, you or the school may initiate the evaluation process (see Figure 2). If you are concerned that your child may have a disability and need services, you should reach out to the school. You can start with your child's teacher, or you can schedule a meeting with the principal, counselor, or special education chair of your child's school or district. You can even start this process before your child is school-aged. Children must be at least 3 years old to qualify for an IEP. However, children from birth to age 3 may also qualify for services through an Individualized Family Service Plan (IFSP). For very young children, you can start by reaching out to your public school district or to your state's early childhood or early intervention programs. The 2004 reauthorization of IDEA increased supports for early intervention. I recommend reaching out in writing (e-mail is fine) and also in person or over the phone.

Although the school personnel must take your request seriously, they are not legally obligated to honor the request if they disagree with it. If they disagree with your request, they must say why they disagree in writing (this is called giving *prior written notice*; see Figure 3). If this happens, you do have recourse. You can take some of the steps outlined in "Next Steps If You Disagree With the Decision" (p. 38). You can also schedule a meeting with the district administrative team and/or reach out to parent

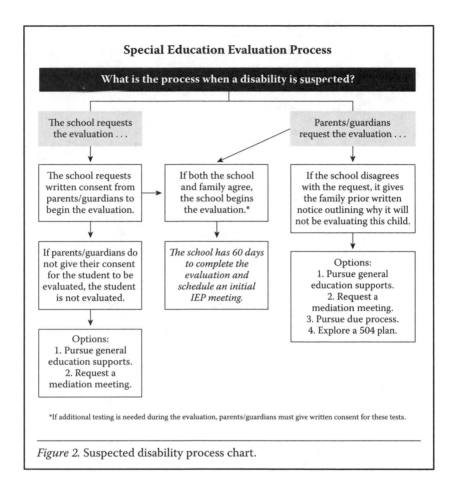

Figure 2. Suspected disability process chart.

advocacy groups for students with disabilities. If you don't know where to find a parent advocacy group, research information on your state Parent Training and Information Center (PTI). If the members of the school team agree with your request, they will ask for your consent to evaluate your child. Once you give consent, the school has 60 days to complete the evaluation, and all results must be shared with you at an initial or eligibility IEP meeting.

The school can also initiate the eligibility process. If school personnel initiate the request to have your child evaluated, they must ask your permission. When you receive this request, you may experience a wide range of emotions. You might worry about stigma and labeling. You might feel shame for reasons you can't fully articulate. You might want to pro-

---

Special Education and Prior Written Notice

How does prior written notice (PWN) work?

What is it? PWN is a communication tool between the school and parents/guardians. Requirements for prior written notice are outlined in IDEA.

When is it needed? PWN is required in all of the situations outline below.

Evaluation	**Placement**	**Services**
When an evaluation is requested or denied by the school.	When an educational placement change is suggested or denied by the school.	When a change in services is suggested or denied by the school.

Identification
When there has been a change in identification (disability category) or eligibility for special education services.

What needs to be included? PWNs that describe actions the school is refusing should clearly delineate what was proposed, why it is being refused, and what evidence was used to make this decision.

What if we haven't been given PWN? If you have requested an evaluation, change in placement, or change in services, and the school declines but does not provide you with a PWN, request one.

What should we do with the PWNs we receive? Prior written notice creates a written record of changes proposed or denied in your child's education plan. Keep all of these notices for reference or in the case of a dispute.

Figure 3. Understanding prior written notice.

---

tect your child by disagreeing with the suggestion that they could have a disability. You might agree and still feel embarrassed, worried, or sad. You might agree and feel relieved to be on the path to some answers for why your child is struggling in school. You might agree and feel neutral based on past experiences or because you were wondering the same thing. You might feel all of these conflicting emotions simultaneously. Or you might feel none of these. Parenting decisions are complex. If you are having a hard time with the decision, give yourself some grace (see Chapter 8) and seek more information. A disability—if one is identified—won't define your child. Learn more about the special education services at your child's school. Remember, the policy victories for inclusion are relatively recent—special education services likely look a lot different than when you attended school. Remember that if you agree to an evaluation, you aren't yet agreeing to a service plan. You'll have time to review the results of the evaluation with the school team and make decisions about what supports are or are not appropriate for your child.

An evaluation also doesn't represent a static judgment on who your child is; instead it is an information-gathering process that will help build targeted supports in the future. If you give your consent to have your child evaluated, the school has 60 days to complete the evaluation. As part of IDEA, this evaluation is done without cost to you. Your child will be evaluated to determine whether or not a disability is present and what (if any) services may help support their learning. Special education evaluations are multifaceted. Depending on the challenges your child is exhibiting, the school may also review your child's health, vision, hearing, and medical records for additional information. The evaluation team may ask you to complete surveys about your child's social-emotional and practical functioning. These surveys might also be completed by teachers and others who know your child well. The team will likely review your child's current schoolwork. Intelligence, aptitude, and language tests may be administered as well. Each evaluation should be individualized to your child's unique situation and comprehensive enough to give the team the information needed to determine (1) if a disability is present and (2) what services (if any) might support the child. The results of this evaluation will be shared with you at an initial or eligibility IEP evaluation meeting (see Chapter 3).

In sharing these results, the school team will likely talk about ranges and continuums. There is a range of ability/disability and a continuum of services to meet students' diverse needs. No two children are alike, including children who are identified with the same disability. Parents often know this best. Figure 4 outlines some terms you might hear around disability. The IEP team might refer to your child's disability as mild, moderate, or profound.

Once the initial evaluation has been conducted, the results will be shared and explained to you at your initial or eligibility IEP meeting. If a disability is identified, this will likely be the first of at least annual IEP meetings. However, what do we do if a disability is not identified?

Range of Disabilities *Both ability and placement are malleable.*		
Mild	**Moderate**	**Profound**
If your child spends most of the educational day in the general education classroom, their disability may be referred to as mild. These students can function within a general classroom setting with accommodations.	If your child receives special education services throughout the school day with limited access to general education classrooms, their disability may be referred to as moderate. These students generally need accommodations, modifications, and additional special education services to function within a general classroom setting.	If your child receives special education services for all or nearly all of their school day, their disability may be referred to as profound (or sometimes, severe). These students need a range of supports to access the general education school setting, often including a paraprofessional to work one-on-one with them.
Many factors contribute to a student's ability to access the general education classroom. These factors can change over the course of a student's life based on personal growth as well as school or family-based interventions and support. Further, the disability category does not always tell us whether that disability currently manifests as mild, moderate, or profound. For example, one student on the autism spectrum may spend most of their time in a general education classroom, while another student also on the autism spectrum may require the supports of the special education classroom for most of the school day.		

Figure 4. Range of disabilities.

What If My Child Doesn't Qualify for Special Education Services?

The school team might determine that your child does not qualify for an IEP. This means the school does not have enough evidence to support that your child has a disability covered by IDEA and/or that your child does not demonstrate a need for educational interventions in order to achieve at school. This can be frustrating. You or the school thought your child needed the support of special education; you went through the process of an evaluation, and this wasn't the outcome you expected. Where do you go from here? You have recourse and some good options to consider. Let's talk about them.

The first step is to gather relevant information from this recent evaluation and determination. You have the right to see the results from your child's evaluation and have those explained to you. You also have the right to a clear explanation (in writing) as to why your child did not qualify for special education services. Both of these usually happen at the initial or eligibility IEP meeting. However, if they do not, you can (and should) request them. I'd recommend making your request in writing (over e-mail is fine). Following up in person is also a good idea. Once you have this information, you can (1) agree with it and pursue other support plans, both inside and outside of school, or (2) disagree with it and pursue other evaluations or a more formal dispute. We'll talk about each of these options briefly. Whichever you decide, I'd recommend keeping a paper trail of your child's progress over the next academic year. Keep e-mails, report cards, classroom tests, and work samples that illustrate your child's challenges in school. Also keep examples that illustrate your child's strengths. All support plans should include both challenges and strengths. These examples will help you whether you choose to develop a support plan without special services or use them to build a case for a reevaluation.

Next Steps If You Agree With the Decision

The school used a team of experts to evaluate your child. It's possible that your child struggles (with or without a disability) but legitimately does not qualify for services under IDEA. If you agree with this determination, you have three options and you can use them individually or in combination.

First, you can pursue in-school supports. Even without an IEP, the mission of school is to serve all students. Ask for a meeting with your child's teacher(s), counselor, and administrator to brainstorm support strategies, including appropriate accommodations (see Figure 11 on p. 64). Sometimes these supports include breaking down big tasks, giving more frequent breaks, setting up an incentive system, providing a safe space to go cool off, or having students work with a school tutor. These ideas should be individualized to your child's needs, may require some creativity, and will likely need fine-tuning until you have a plan that works.

Next, you can pursue out-of-school supports. These might include outside tutoring, meeting with a therapist (social-emotional, speech, or OT), brainstorming with a coach or religious leader, and setting up an incentive system at home. Note that although you may be able to find some community-based lower cost options, these out-of-school therapies are sometimes expensive. Reach out to your community and see what options are available.

Finally, you can pursue a 504 plan. More information about Section 504 is included at the end of this chapter.

Next Steps If You Disagree With the Decision

If you disagree with the decision, you also have some options. (For additional background on your rights and safeguards see Figure 8 on p. 48.) You can request a *mediation meeting*. Mediation meetings are covered under IDEA. At a mediation meeting, a *neutral professional* will listen to both sides and try to help you arrive at a workable solution. School districts maintain a list of qualified mediators who are well-versed in the particularities of special education policy. Mediators are compensated by state funding in order to ensure that mediation is free to both families and school districts. You may also choose to bring your lawyer to a mediation meeting; the school may choose to have its counsel present as well. Generally, if one group brings an attorney, it is advisable for the other to do the same. Legal counsel is not always necessary or even advisable in an early meeting. It is just fine for both parties to try to work toward a resolution without lawyers present. Another option, in addition to or instead of mediation, is to do your own evaluation. This is called an *independent educational evaluation* (IEE). Although schools will not pay for this additional evaluation, the results can help you contest their decision. Finally, you can take litigative action through either *due process* or a *state complaint*. If going this route, you will definitely want to seek counsel through an educational attorney.

You don't have to navigate the process of disagreeing on your own. There are formal and informal supports available to you. First, each state has a Parent Training and Information Center (PTI). The PTI's primary purpose is to help parents of children with disabilities navigate the school process. Sometimes it is a little tricky to locate your state PTI, as different states call this group by different names. Some states have both state-level PTIs and local groups working toward the same mission. Searching online for "all state PTIs" will give you a good starting place. Your state department of education should be able to help you as well. Use your own support networks. See if there is a parent group for families of children with disabilities. If applicable, reach out to your religious community or neighborhood groups.

Another option is to get the help of an educational advocate or educational attorney. There is usually a fee for these services. If the cost is prohibitive for you, sometimes advocates will take on cases pro bono. Legal aid offices can sometimes help, too. Again, if you are considering pursuing due process or a state complaint, you'll want to work directly with your own legal counsel.

Whether you agree or disagree with the school's evaluation, if your child does not qualify for services under IDEA and is still struggling in school, a common next step is to explore a 504 plan. If a child qualifies under Section 504, this can be an effective alternate route for getting services and setting up a success plan. The following section gives background on 504 plans. If your child already qualifies for an IEP, you may want to skip ahead to Chapter 3, which covers IEPs in detail.

Understanding Section 504

Remember how the ADA and IDEA define disability in slightly different terms? The special education evaluation outlined in the previous section used IDEA's definition. Section 504 uses the broader definition outlined in the ADA. Section 504 is part of the policy victories shared at the beginning of this chapter. If your child does not qualify for an IEP, the school team might mention a 504 plan as an alternative. If the school team doesn't mention this, you can ask about it. Let's step back and learn a little about Section 504 (Disability Rights Education and Defense Fund, n.d.):

> Section 504 of the 1973 Rehabilitation Act was the first disability civil rights law to be enacted in the United States. It prohibits discrimination against people with disabilities in programs that receive federal financial assistance, and set the stage for enactment of the Americans with Disabilities Act. Section 504 works together with the ADA and IDEA to protect children

and adults with disabilities from exclusion, and unequal
treatment in schools, jobs and the community. (para. 1)

All children with disabilities (including those who qualify for IEPs)
are protected by the ADA, which was informed by Section 504. As a civil
rights statute, Section 504 requires that the needs of students with disabilities be met as adequately as the needs of the general student population.
If a child qualifies for an IEP under IDEA, the IEP document outlines the
ways in which the student's unique needs will be met. If a child does not
qualify for an IEP—or, in rare cases, in conjunction with an IEP—a 504
plan may serve a similar purpose. It is unusual to have both an IEP and 504
plan, as having an IEP usually makes the 504 plan redundant. The exception is when a student's disabilities are addressed in an IEP but their additional medical needs (temporary or chronic) are not addressed in the IEP.

To qualify for services under Section 504, a child must "have a physical or mental impairment that substantially limits one or more major life
activities" (Office for Civil Rights, 2018). The evaluation process for determining this impairment is more streamlined than the IEP evaluation. In
fact, it's possible, given the recent IEP evaluation, that the school will have
all of the information needed to make a 504 determination and plan. If you
want to add more information to the evaluation folder, you can also include
medical records and other information from teachers and those who know
your child well. For example, you might want to include an ADHD or other
diagnosis from your pediatrician if relevant. If the school doesn't suggest
a 504 plan at your initial IEP, ask who the school 504 coordinator is and
request (in writing) an evaluation for a 504 plan.

Section 504 requires that students with disabilities be given appropriate education just like their general education peers; 504 plans explain
how a school intends to do that. Although 504 *protections* are regulated
by federal law, 504 *plans* are not an official part of this legislation. The law
says that all children are entitled to free and appropriate educational services. However, Section 504 does not outline how schools will deliver such
services. This leads to some discrepancies in how different schools author
and regulate these plans. 504 plans often include accommodations and
modifications (see Figure 11 on p. 64), as well as related services, such
as working with an SLP, OT, or PT. Just as we do with IEPs, a best practice
is to have the 504 plan reviewed and updated annually.

Throughout this chapter, I've intentionally framed inclusion as a civil
right. We've unpacked some of the policy language that protects children

with disabilities and talked about what a disability can and cannot tell us. We also explored different scenarios that might happen when a disability is suspected. Finally, we reviewed what next steps you have if your child doesn't qualify for services under IDEA. Now let's explore what happens if your child does qualify for services under IDEA. If your child qualifies for these services, you will attend at least annual IEP meetings. In the next chapter, we'll explore the IEP process at greater length.

Chapter 3

IEP Overview

An *Individualized Education Program* (IEP) outlines the goals and supports for children who qualify for special education services. An IEP team is made up of people invested in your child's educational success. In this chapter, I'll talk through strategies for working together as an IEP team; I'll review what each of the different agenda items means so you know what to expect; and I'll share times when I think it is important and worthwhile to pause the meeting and ask for more clarification or to take things in a different direction.

In brief, the IEP is a legally binding document that reviews the services, goals, accommodations, and modifications[5] that a student will receive to meet their educational needs in a public schools. It also includes background information and, in the case of students 16 years old and older, transition plans for after high school. This document is updated at least annually, although it can be updated more frequently at the request of any member of the IEP team, including parents. It must also be updated whenever there is a change to a student's needs or services. See Figure 5 for more information about when IEP meetings are scheduled.

IEP meetings can feel confusing and even intimidating. However, with more information about the purpose, policies, and structures of the meeting beforehand, you'll be able to approach these conversations with greater confidence. Let's talk through what your family can expect at an IEP meeting.

---

5 For more information on the differences between accommodations and modifications, see Figure 11 (p. 64).

How Are IEP Meetings Scheduled?

Meetings Are Scheduled by the School

IDEA requires that all IEP meetings be scheduled to accommodate parent/guardian participation. This means:
> giving adequate advanced notice,
> scheduling meetings at a mutually agreeable time and place, and
> notifying families of everyone who is invited to the meeting.

Meetings Can Be Requested by the Family

Although schools typically initiate IEP meeting requests, parents/guardians may also request an IEP meeting outside of this schedule. Do so in writing, clearing explaining why you think an IEP meeting is needed.
The school is required to respond to your request. Timelines for responding vary by state.

Four Types of IEP Meetings

Initial IEP meeting	Annual IEP meeting	Triennial IEP meeting	Other IEP meetings > Discuss transition > Discuss behavior > Discuss change in services

---

An IEP Is Not the Only Kind of School Meeting

If your child is in an emergency situation, particularly around safety, it is often faster to work with the school or district to schedule a meeting outside of the formal IEP process.

Figure 5. Scheduling IEP meetings.

Family Expectations for IEP Meetings

For many students with disabilities, the IEP is the cornerstone document outlining their educational support plans. IEP meetings happen at least annually. Over the next several sections, I'll walk through some of the specific things you can expect during your IEP meetings and offer tools to help you advocate for goals and plans that are proactive and relevant to your exceptional child. When going into an IEP meeting, you can expect long documents, policy and procedural language, and more talking about your child's disability than you are likely comfortable with. You can also expect useful information, conversations with professionals who work directly with your child, and the opportunity to get many of your questions about services and support plans answered. The official IEP document ranges from 15–50 pages. It can feel intimidating to see such a lengthy document about your child and to then have to discuss it, particularly the nuances of your child's disability, in a 1–2 hour meeting with teachers, counselors, and others present. That overwhelming feeling is normal, and it is also perfectly okay to pause the meeting at any point and ask questions when something is unclear.

Let's review the typical agenda of an IEP meeting. The person chairing the meeting, often your child's case manager or learning specialist, may prepare an agenda for participants. Whether or not the chair gives you a printed agenda, most IEPs follow the format outlined in Figure 6.

Introductions and Purpose

There will probably be many people around the table at an IEP meeting, including a special education teacher, general education teacher, counselor, principal, school psychologist, related services providers, you (and possibly your partner[6]), and even your child. Everyone at the meeting should know how each person is connected to your child[7]. The IEP meeting should start with introductions; however, if it doesn't, you can choose to initiate these introductions by extending your hand to someone across the table and identifying yourself as a parent. This should cue the rest of the group to make formal introductions.

There are several reasons to hold an IEP meeting. Figure 7 explains the different types of IEP meetings, their purposes, and how often these meetings are held.

---

6 Often one parent bears the burden of attending IEP meetings alone. Knowing how emotionally charged and difficult these meetings can be, it can be helpful to arrange schedules so that you and your partner or another important adult in your child's life can attend IEP meetings together. You'll often hear different things, ask different questions, and bring different perspectives to the table.

7 Older children (teenagers) are asked to participate in their IEPs, particularly to share their thoughts on transition planning and goals. See Chapter 5 for more information on transition plans. Depending on you and your child's preferences, younger children may also attend and participate in IEPs.

Sample IEP Meeting Agenda

> Introductions
> Purpose and norms (e.g., eligibility, annual review, change in services)
> Parent rights
> Present levels of performance
>> Assessment reports
>> General education teacher
>> Special education specialist
>> School psychologist
>> Other specialists (e.g., SLP, OT, PT)

> Eligibility determination (initial and triennial meetings only)
> Annual goals
> Services
>> Accommodations/modifications
>> Placement

> Transition plan (if student is over 16)
> Meeting summary, questions/answers
> Signatures

Figure 6. Sample IEP meeting agenda.

Parent and Guardian Rights

IDEA requires that parents/guardians are presented with procedural rights and safeguards annually. To achieve the yearly requirement, most schools give a copy of the procedural rights and safeguards to you at your annual IEP. They are a thick packet written in legal language. Often there is little explanation of what the rights and safeguards mean; instead parents and guardians simply sign that they *received* them. Knowing your rights is incredibly important; therefore, in Figure 8, I summarize what the procedural rights and safeguards mean, so that when you are presented with them at the meeting, you can understand the purpose of these powerful legislative reminders (Lee, 2019).

In summary, the procedural rights and safeguards ensure that you are a critical decision maker in your child's educational plan. You have the right to understand all information presented about your child, all services proposed for your child, and all of your rights. Your consent is necessary

IEP Meeting Type	Primary Purpose	Frequency
Initial (or eligibility) IEP meeting	Discuss eligibility and services.	Once
Annual IEP meeting	Review progress and services, and set goals.	Annually
Triennial IEP meeting	Discuss if your child continues to qualify for special education services and, if so, what those services should be. Testing and review of current data, similar to what was conducted for the initial meeting, are done in preparation for this triennial meeting.	Every 3 years
Additional IEPs	Discuss changes in services or needs.	As needed

Figure 7. Types of IEP meetings.

for an evaluation or services. You also have the right to disagree with decisions made about your child, and there is a formal process to settle these disagreements. You might think of it like this: *These procedures safeguard that your child's rights are affirmed and honored in the school setting, and they further outline the procedures necessary for consent of services/evaluation or dispute.* You may request another copy of the procedural rights and safeguards anytime you need. If your home language is not English, your school district is required to help you find a copy or translation of the procedural rights and safeguards in your home language.

When children reach the *age of majority*, the age that begins adulthood as determined by your state, they will typically take on the educational rights previously held by their parents/guardians. In most states, 18 years old is the age of majority, but in some states children are not considered adults until they reach 21. The year before your child reaches the age of majority, the school should let your family know which rights will transfer to your child. These rights usually include an obligation to participate in all IEP meetings, give consent for educational evaluation, sign off on changes to services or placement, and give consent for parents to be

	Right/Safeguard	Implications
1	Access to educational records	You have the right to see and receive a copy of all of your child's educational records.
2	Independent educational evaluation (IEE)	You have the right to an outside (nonschool) evaluation, and the school is required to consider these results. (*Note.* "Consider" does not mean act on.)
3	Parent/guardian participation	You have a legal right to participate in your child's educational decision making, including being part of the IEP team.
4	Prior written notice	Before adding, changing, removing, or denying services to your child, the school must notify you in writing.
5	Procedural safeguards notice	You must be given a copy of these legal rights and safeguards.
6	Understandable language	You have a right to understand what you are consenting to or being given notice of. This means that you are entitled to explanations in accessible language. (*Note.* This includes having documents translated into your home language.)
7	Confidentiality	Your child's personal identifiable information, such as name, address, social security number, and other personal details, is to be kept confidential. The Family Educational Rights and Privacy Act of 1974 outlines these protections and their exceptions.
8	Informed consent	Evaluations and special education services cannot be provided without your prior written consent.
9	Right to "stay put"	If you are going through a dispute with the school over services, your child has the right to stay in their current placement (school/services) until that dispute is settled.

Figure 8. Understanding procedural rights and safeguards (Lee, 2019).

	Right/Safeguard	Implications
10	Due process	You have a right to dispute decisions made about your child's education. To do so, you will file a written complaint. Within 15 days of this complaint, you and the school will hold a resolution session, followed by a due process hearing. It is often a good idea to hire legal representation for these meetings.
11	Civil action	Your next step, should you disagree with the results of the due process hearing, is to file a civil lawsuit. It is advisable to hire legal representation for this lawsuit.
12	Mediation	You also have the right to try to settle disagreements outside of the legal process, through a mediation meeting, which happens within the school and is facilitated by a neutral third party. Many families choose to bring an advocate to mediation meetings.
13	Reimbursement of legal fees	If you win a due process hearing or civil lawsuit, a judge or hearing officer may order that the school reimburse your legal fees.
14	State-level appeal	This state-dependent safeguard grants families in some states the right to appeal due process decisions to the state department of education.
15	State complaint	If you believe the school has violated state or federal law in its services (or lack of services) for your child, you may submit a complaint to an official state agency. You may write this complaint yourself or ask for an advocate to help you.

Figure 8. Continued.

invited and included in the IEP meetings[8]. I recommend including your child in the IEP process well before the age of majority. After all, the plans, goals, and services you are discussing ultimately are your child's.

8 If your child is not able to take over these responsibilities, you can explore *guardianship* with an attorney. If granted, this would allow you to continue in your role as the educational decision maker and provider of informed consent. This is a legal process that happens outside of school.

Present Levels of Performance

In order to develop support plans that help your child grow, learn, and achieve at higher levels, you must know where your child is currently performing. This is the purpose of the *Present Level of Performance* (PLOP), known also in some districts as the *Present Level of Educational Performance* (PLEP)[9]. This is a summary statement about what your child is able to do in school, and it is used to help the team understand at what level a child is currently performing (in their area of need). PLOP gives the team a starting place and important data to write meaningful goals, which we'll cover in a moment.

IDEA requires that present levels include statements on your child's (1) academic achievement and (2) functional performance. Functional performance refers to nonacademic skills necessary for functioning at school and/or in life, such as:

›   social development,
›   physical/health development,
›   executive/management needs, and
›   communication.

Additionally, present levels should address how the child's disability (or area of need) affects involvement in the general education curriculum or, for preschool children, in "appropriate activities."

Present level statements are written based on a review of multiple data sources, including assessment, review of student work/observation, reports from any stakeholders in the child's IEP team, and formal evaluation tools. Usually present levels are written in data-based language in which tasks and achievement are quantified. These kinds of statements may feel odd or cold. We rarely talk about our children using this sort of language. For example, when asked about bedtime at my house, I would never say, "My daughter is working on taking charge of her bedtime routine. Right now she brushes her teeth without prompting 70% of the time, with 80% accuracy, often missing her back teeth." Instead, I would probably say, "She does an okay job brushing her teeth even without my asking; however, some nights are a struggle." Although the second statement gives you a picture of what teeth brushing looks like at our house, it isn't mea-

---

9 Colloquially teachers in special education often refer to these by their acronyms; both PLEP and PLOP are pronounced as words.

surable or specific. Four weeks from now, if you ask how things are going, I won't have much to say. Maybe it's going "a little better" or "a little worse." Without some benchmarks, I'll probably tell you it's "about the same." This isn't a lot of help in tracking or supporting my daughter's progress.

When present level statements are shared, the IEP team should give you an overview of what data were used to make these determinations. For example, the team members might share assessment reports, survey or anecdotal information from the general education teacher, survey or anecdotal information from a learning specialist, results of any assessments (formal or informal) conducted by the school psychologist, student work samples, and reports or samples from other specialists (e.g., SLP, OT, PT). If you don't understand what information was used to make determinations, or if it isn't shared, ask for another explanation. The IEP team members should help you understand how they arrived at these statements.

Present level statements should give clear information about what a child is working on, particularly any areas of concern. Remember, you know your child better than anyone else in the room. If the PLOP doesn't ring true, speak up. For example, one year my family's IEP team brought up some concerns with reading comprehension. At home, our son was reading novels several grades above his age level. Unless we told him he had to go to sleep, he would read late into the night. He could (and would!) enthusiastically tell us about the complicated plots of the exciting stories he was reading. When I shared this at our IEP meeting, the conversation shifted. Perhaps reading comprehension wasn't the challenge. Maybe the challenges the school was seeing stemmed instead from too little choice in reading, or from concerns with attention and executive functioning[10]. Share your impressions, observations, and questions with the IEP team. This dialogue will lead to more accurate summaries and more meaningful goals.

Because present levels are written based on your child's area of need, the focus often seems to be on what your child can't do (yet). This can feel discouraging. If you are feeling discouraged during the present levels part of the IEP, pause the meeting and help everyone reframe the conversation.

---

10 Executive functioning refers to the ability to manage oneself and one's resources. Organization, advanced planning, and keeping track of materials are often addressed under the executive functioning umbrella.

Let me give you an example. A team might share a PLOP such as this one:

> Owen has been working on letter sounds. On three out of four attempts, he was able to give the sounds of 60% of the alphabet letters, including short and long vowel sounds. He missed b, d, l, r, y, u, q, c, and t.

In this case, it is completely appropriate to stop and celebrate that Owen can now name 60% of the alphabet sounds. Maybe last year he wasn't yet recognizing letter names. Maybe 2 months ago he was struggling to remember the sounds in his own name, and this time you notice he correctly identified all of the sounds in O-w-e-n. Has the IEP team talked about Owen's motivation to learn to read? Maybe Owen loves books. Perhaps he carries them around the house, reciting his favorites and asking you to read to him over and over again. If so, this information about his motivation is important; after all, the reason Owen is working on letter sounds is to support reading. Ask the team to add a sentence to the PLOP, saying something like, "Owen is very motivated to learn how to read."

Others on the IEP team will have celebrations to share, too. When they do, soak them up. If the IEP members don't share these readily, prompt them to do so. Ask the teachers and specialists what growth they have noticed in your child's learning. Ask the team members to share the strengths they see in the classroom. If needed, you can help everyone at the meeting remember that Owen is doing his best and that his progress is not only worth acknowledging but also worth celebrating.

Because the present levels, goals, and IEP are largely focused on disability and success planning around the areas of struggle for our children, sometimes the overall tone can feel negative. It is always okay to pause the meeting and say something like, "Whoa, this is feeling discouraging! Let's spend a few minutes talking about what Ann/John/Lacy/Demarco *can* do." Yes, this takes courage and can feel uncomfortable. I encourage you to do so anyhow! Shifting the conversation to a strengths-based dialogue is important for your child's success. Overwhelmingly, the IEP team should hear you and be glad to offer plenty of anecdotes and data on your child's strengths. These anecdotes should also be part of the narrative of the IEP. The most useful present levels include information about strengths and how children learn best. The most effective success plans celebrate and leverage our children's strengths.

Eligibility Determination

Determining initial eligibility was covered at length in Chapter 2. I know it's a lot of information! Let me summarize briefly, and then, if you would like a longer refresher, feel free to flip back to Chapter 2 to review in more detail. According to IDEA, a student must have a "disabling condition" to qualify for special education services (see Figure 9 on pp. 57–59 for the 13 "disabling conditions" recognized by IDEA). Further, this disability must have an "adverse effect" on the child's "education"; both of these terms are open to some interpretation. Eligibility is typically discussed during an IEP meeting in three cases:

> initial or eligibility IEP meetings,
> triennial meetings, and
> as requested by members of the IEP team.

The following paragraphs offer more information about these second two cases.

IDEA requires a *triennial reevaluation* every 3 years. However, parents or school personnel may also notice changes in a child's abilities, challenges, and areas of need, and request a reevaluation sooner. The purpose of any reevaluation is to assess a child's needs, including gathering information to determine whether or not those needs have changed, and determining whether or not the child still qualifies for (and needs) special education services.

The first step in a reevaluation is a *review of existing information*; this includes all previous evaluations, student work samples, observations, and reports from specialists, as well as information from general education teachers and learning specialists. After this review, the IEP team has a lot of latitude to consider what data sources are necessary to make these determinations. For example, if there is already enough information to confirm eligibility and services for your child, formal testing may not be required.

Formal Assessments and Reevaluation

If the school team decides that additional formal assessments are needed, you will have to consent in writing to the additional testing before it can happen. If you believe additional formal assessments are necessary and the school team disagrees, the school is not obligated to honor your request unless it is terminating all services. If your child is continuing to receive special education services, and you believe additional formal assessment is necessary but the school disagrees, you have a few options:

› *Let it go.* This happened to my family once. In my opinion, the formal assessments from previous reevaluations (6 years prior) no longer seemed accurate regarding our son's language arts skills, particularly in reading comprehension and vocabulary. I wanted him retested so that his record would show what I was certain would be higher percentiles. The school personnel said this was unnecessary; he continued to qualify for services, and his disability category wasn't changing. At the end of the day, I saw their point, in part. Additional formal testing wasn't going to have tangible benefits for our son. Without more to gain, I let it go.

› *Independent educational evaluation (IEE).* You have the right to pursue an IEE, or "outside evaluation." If you want to pursue this option, your local parent-teacher organization (PTO) or school district should have a list of evaluators to recommend and information on costs for these evaluations. You are not required to choose from this list. If you have a compelling reason to go with another evaluator, you are welcome to do so. The list is generally a good starting place though, as these evaluators have typically been vetted and well-trained.

› *Exercise your due process rights.* As this is the most extreme option, I recommend seeking thoughtful counsel on how and when to pursue it. You might consider this if (1) you have requested reevaluation and been denied before, (2) if other attempts at mediation have not worked, and (3) if you believe your child is being harmed by not receiving services. (See p. 49 for more information on due process.)

Remember that testing only tells one part of your child's story, and that story is limited at best. Provided that your child is receiving the services needed to be successful, and provided that the IEP feels accurate, formal testing may or may not be essential.

If your child is *not* receiving the services needed, or if the school district has determined that your child no longer qualifies for any special education services, then you may want to insist on additional testing. In fact, if your child no longer qualifies for special education services, and (1) you disagree and (2) no formal testing was done to make this determination, then you can request a formal assessment. The district is obligated to honor that request.

Determining Category

Before I explain the 13 disability categories covered under IDEA, I want to circle back to our earlier discussion about what a disability does and doesn't tell us. Disability may be one part of your child's identity. Like all identities, there are times when disability feels front and center to you and your child's experience, and there are other times when it seems not as important. Disability doesn't tell us about your child's character, interests, or what your child will or will not accomplish. In fact, some people claim (and I have seen firsthand) that individuals with disabilities sometimes have increased capabilities, talents, and strengths *because of*, not in spite of, their disabilities. We'll talk more about this exciting topic in Chapter 7.

The presence of a disability tells us a bit about the kinds of supports, accommodations, or modifications a student is likely to need in school. This information can help with support planning. IDEA says that a child may only qualify for services under one disability category. This is sometimes confusing and/or contentious[11]. Let's talk about what this means and what it doesn't. This means that students can only qualify for special education services under one disability category. This does not mean a child can only have one disability. For example, a child may be blind and also have autism, or a child may have a specific learning disability and also have an orthopedic impairment (e.g., cerebral palsy). *Multiple disabilities* is a category that may be used in extenuating cases, defined by IDEA as multiple "impairments . . . the combination of which causes such severe educational needs that they cannot be accommodated in a special education program solely for one of the impairments."[12] In most cases, the IEP team will identify the one category that is primarily complicating academic performance. Any additional disabilities or challenges should also be well-documented in the IEP and considered in the student's success plan.

With this background, let's spend a little time exploring the disability categories under IDEA. Some of you may have been familiar with the language around your child's disability since early childhood. For others, all

---

11 To read the law, refer to IDEA section 300.641(c).

12 Deaf-blindness is not documented as a "multiple disability" as it has its own unique disability category.

of these terms are new, unfamiliar, and possibly confusing. For example, approximately half of all students who receive special education services qualify under "specific learning disabilities" (Special Education Guide, 2019). I often joke that the term *specific learning disabilities* isn't very—ahem—specific. Figure 9 is a chart to help with some preliminary information about the 13 disability categories.

The information in this chart is informed by how IDEA defines these categories and may differ from medical, psychological, or other definitions. Even with these definitions, there is still room for ambiguity and nuance among the categories. In terms of determining a disability category for special education services, remember that the most important consideration is how (and if) a disability adversely affects educational performance.

Annual Goals

The annual goals in your child's IEP should be closely linked to present levels of performance (see p. 50). The PLOP outlines what your child is working on and currently able to do; the annual goal should outline how your child will improve on these skills over the next school year. These goals should be SMART: specific, measurable, attainable, relevant, and time-bound. Typically IEP goals follow a formula that goes something like this:

> By [*date*], [*student name*] will [*specific action/skill*] as measured by [*specific objectives or markers*] with [*% accuracy*] on [*frequency or number of trials*].

In my experience, many learning specialists are experts at writing specific, measurable, attainable, and time-bound goals. But what's missing from this formula?

That's right—relevance. I've sat through a lot of IEP meetings in which the goals perfectly follow the formula but don't matter that much to the child personally or to the child's overall success in school. Who is the best person to comment on how relevant a goal is? The student! When included in the process, students often have powerful perspectives about how relevant and motivating certain goals are or are not. If the student cannot be included in the IEP meeting, a family member is often the second best person to comment on the goals. We need IEP goals that matter

13 Disability Categories Covered Under IDEA		
Disability Category	**Acronym**	**Potential Educational Impacts**
Autism Autism spectrum disorders represent a developmental disability that has a significant impact on communication and social interaction.	ASD	Challenges with verbal/ nonverbal communication and social interaction; specialized interests are also common.
Deaf-blindness Combined hearing and visual impairments.	D/B	Severe communication, development, and educational needs that cannot be addressed by services or programs specific to students with only blindness or deafness.
Deafness A severe hearing impairment.	D	Challenges or an inability to process auditory/linguistic information through hearing.
Emotional disturbance An umbrella term used to refer to mental health and behavioral challenges that adversely affect a child's education.	ED	Needs in learning (not explained by other factors), interpersonal relationships, appropriate school behaviors, and mental health.
Hearing impairment An impairment in hearing not covered under deafness; may be permanent or fluctuating.	HH	Challenges or an inability to process auditory/linguistic information through hearing.
Intellectual disability[1] Severe limitations in intellectual and behavioral functioning, as determined by IQ and a person's ability to engage in independent behaviors.	ID	Learning challenges (across subjects), behavioral challenges (particularly when completing tasks independently), and struggles with complex (multistep) tasks.

1 This disability category was formerly called "mental retardation" (MR). Although this term is outdated and no longer included in IDEA, you may still come across it. Feel free to educate others about more appropriate ways to refer to individuals with cognitive/intellectual disabilities.

Figure 9. Understanding disability categories under IDEA.

13 Disability Categories Covered Under IDEA		
Disability Category	**Acronym**	**Potential Educational Impacts**
Multiple disabilities Concurrent disabilities (besides deaf-blindness) that cause educational challenges that cannot be addressed with services or programs for only one disability.	MD[2]	Because the possible combinations are so varied, many different challenges may be present; in particular, it can be complicated to find the appropriate educational setting for your child to learn in.
Orthopedic impairment Physical disabilities that impact/impede a child's educational progress.	OI	An umbrella category that represents a considerable diversity of needs; often for students with physical disabilities, IEP teams work on communication, physical access of school spaces, adaptive PE, and health needs that interfere with learning.
Other health impairment Chronic health challenges, such as asthma, Attention Deficit/Hyperactivity Disorder (ADHD), diabetes, epilepsy, a heart condition, hemophilia, lead poisoning, leukemia, nephritis, rheumatic fever, sickle cell anemia, and Tourette syndrome, that adversely affect a child's educational performance.[3]	OHI	Another umbrella term for many health needs; students in this category have a variety of educational challenges often including focus, attention, and ability to attend to school tasks; ADHD is currently the biggest category of students under the OHI category.

2 You may also see MH for multiple handicapped; this term is less often used and less appropriate.

3 Depending on the educational needs of a child in this and other categories, they (1) may qualify for an IEP (2) qualify for a 504 Plan, or (3) only need a health plan with a nurse.

Figure 9. Continued.

13 Disability Categories Covered Under IDEA		
Disability Category	Acronym	Potential Educational Impacts
Specific learning disability A disability that cannot be explained by any of the other disability categories and impacts reading, writing, listening, speaking, or calculating.	SLD	Difficulty performing academic tasks in the child's disability area; although children with specific learning disabilities may struggle in one area (e.g., reading or math), they may be quite proficient or even advanced in another.
Speech or language impairment A communication disorder that may include stuttering, articulation, voice, language, or pragmatics, and affects a child's educational progress.	SLI	Challenges with communication, particularly verbal communication, and also nonverbal and pragmatic (social skills).
Traumatic brain injury Severe open or closed head injuries that impede learning.	TBI	Challenges with cognition, language/speech, memory, attention/focus, motor skills, and/or social behavior.
Visual impairment (including blindness) A vision impairment that, even with correction, adversely affects a child's educational performance.	VI	Challenges with visual processing, including reading and accessing text or other visual information, as well as safely accessing the school environment.

Figure 9. Continued.

to our children and support their educational success. It's easy to measure many arbitrary and attainable skills. We want to make sure we are honing skills that directly impact our children's ability to experience success in school and life, even if those skills are harder to measure. If I had to choose between two goals—one that mattered to the student and was very difficult to measure or one that was easily measurable but didn't matter to the student—I'd choose the goal that mattered any day of the week. We don't always have to choose one over the other. With some thoughtfulness, IEP teams can often find goals that are both measurable and relevant.

If the IEP team presents goals that seem too easy or not meaningful enough, say so. Ask the team members:

>   why they chose these goals,
>   how these goals will help your child succeed in school or life, and
>   how they plan to measure continued progress toward these goals.

One strategy IEP teams can use to break down measuring progress toward an IEP goal is to offer specific and relevant objectives. Figure 10 features an example goal for a student. Jim is a high school student who is working on independent living and has a specific learning disability in math. Notice how adding objectives helps everyone understand what this independent living goal will look like and even how it might be taught.

Writing great IEP goals requires the team to identify the meaningful skills a student is working on and to find clear ways to measure progress toward those. At your child's IEP meeting, the team will have proposed goals to share with you. Consider whether or not these goals make sense for your child and will help in meaningful ways. If the goals presented fit this criteria, brainstorm ways to help your child achieve them. If not, speak up. Offer suggestions to improve the goals; maybe that means breaking the goals down to meaningful objectives, or maybe it means suggesting new goals altogether. Your perspective (and your child's perspective when possible) is invaluable.

Services

The services section of the IEP explains how the school or district will support a child's educational progress in the area(s) of concern. This discussion answers two important educational questions:

>   What services or supports will the district provide to help my child succeed in school?
>   How will the school help my child meet individualized educational goals?

These supports generally fit into two different categories: *related services* and *accommodations/modifications*. By writing these services into your child's IEP, the school district is guaranteeing that it will provide these

By May 2019, Jim will be able to successfully use a $10 budget to purchase lunch items at a grocery store as demonstrated by 100% performance for the following steps on three consecutive trials:
1. Selects lunch items (e.g., sandwich, drink, and chips).
2. Verifies that items' total cost is less than $10 (may use a calculator).
3. Locates checkout line.
4. Waits in line appropriately.
5. Takes out money, credit card, or gift card and swipes or hands to cashier.
6. If paying with cash, waits for change.
7. Takes bags and receipt.
8. Says "thank you" to clerk.

Figure 10. Example IEP goal with objectives.

for the next year as long as your child stays in this school[13]. During the IEP meeting, the team will share which related services, if any, your child needs and how those will be provided. The team will then share any accommodations or modifications the school will provide to help your child meet these learning needs and access curriculum.

Related Services

Related services is an umbrella term for additional targeted supports that students may receive to help them meet their learning needs and/or better access the school environment. Typically, these services help children access the general education classroom, curriculum, or environment. If your child does not qualify for an IEP but does qualify for a 504 plan, related services may be part of that plan. If your child needs related services and you are considering a private school instead of a public school, it may still be possible to receive services under an Individual Service Plan (see p. 68). The most common related services include:
> speech and language therapy,
> psychological services,
> occupational therapy,
> physical therapy,

---

13 Students who transfer schools, move out of the district, or attend private school may still be eligible for services, but the process often requires a new IEP or ISP (Individual Support Plan).

> counseling services or social-emotional supports,
> mobility services,
> social work services, and
> school nurse services.

Based on your child's needs and the district's resources, additional services may be included in the plan that are not included in this list. Usually students access these services outside of their classes, often by meeting with a specialist for a one-on-one or small-group session. You may hear these called *pull-out services*.

Depending on the nature of your child's needs, the team may develop a plan that only includes related services, not accommodations or modifications; a combination of related services and accommodations or modifications; or a plan that only includes curricular accommodations or modifications. *Individual* education plans are necessary because students are complex individuals with a variety needs.

Accommodations and Modifications

Accommodations and modifications bridge the gap between the curriculum and your child's learning needs. These can include adjustments to materials, processes, products, and expectations. Although they are similar in nature, accommodations and modifications have some important distinctions. Accommodations change how students learn or how work is presented to them, but do not change expectations or what students learn. Examples of common accommodations teachers might make include:
> reducing the number of items or text on a page,
> providing clear step-by-step written instructions,
> allowing oral responses instead of written responses (when not assessing writing),
> dictating answers to a scribe,
> encouraging spell-check,
> providing a computer for typing notes instead of handwriting,
> allowing a calculator or table for math facts (when not assessing math facts),
> giving exams in a quieter setting and over multiple sessions,
> giving extended time to complete assignments or exams,
> giving frequent breaks between tasks, and
> providing help organizing assignments or deadlines.

Accommodations change *how*, not *what*. You'll notice that for each of the accommodations in this list, *how* information is presented to a student or *how* the student demonstrates mastery is adjusted; however, *what* the student learns does not change. There are countless ways to use accommodations to support student learning.

Families and teachers use accommodations all of the time. We tell a child it is okay to practice counting before going over the ABCs. We fold the tricky homework sheet in half so our 10-year-old only has to look at a half as many problems at a time. We talk through the essay before our seventh grader writes anything down. Teachers and parents constantly adjust process and presentation when work with children. However, there are some accommodations that we don't want to leave up to circumstance. Sometimes there are very specific accommodations that we know can help meet our children's specific needs, and we want to be certain these will be available in every class whenever a child needs them. These are the accommodations we need written into the IEP.

By contrast, modifications change both *how* and *what*. As we move from accommodations to modifications, we might think about moving from smaller adjustments to the curriculum to more significant adjustments (see Figure 11).

Common modifications for students include:
› completing fewer assignments than peers,
› completing different assignments than peers,
› working on different but related skills,
› writing shorter papers or assignments,
› completing an alternative assignment or project,
› responding orally rather than in writing (when writing is assessed),
› using a calculator or table for "math facts" (when math facts are assessed),
› seeing fewer options on multiple-choice exams, and
› being graded on different criteria or a different rubric.

Families and teachers also use modifications all of the time. We tell our children that if they'll just eat their green beans, they don't have to eat their pasta. We tell a struggling student to only complete the first half of the math worksheet. We read a book to a child, instead of the child reading it to us. Modifications are used to meet students where they are while still holding them to high expectations, such as completing work and learning

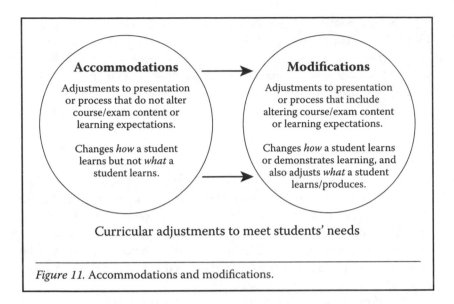

Figure 11. Accommodations and modifications.

material that matches what their peers are learning to the greatest extent possible.

Although accommodations should not change grading scales or how courses are transcripted, occasionally modifications do. Therefore, when the IEP team suggests modifications, or if you think modifications may be needed, be sure to talk through any consequences of changing the curriculum. For example, ask if your child will still be graded on the same grading scale, if your child will still earn credit for the course, how the course will be transcripted, and how results from any alternative or modified assignments will be interpreted.

Accommodations and modifications should be reviewed annually. As we've discussed throughout this book, children's needs often change over time. It is possible that although a child needs a modification now, in a semester or year, that modification will no longer be needed. It's also possible, depending on the nature of your child's needs, that some accommodations or modifications may always be needed in your child's school and work environment. For example, some of our children need assistive technology, voice-to-text software, or adapted PE due to medical or physical differences. Figuring out what works for your child and making sure your child has the right supports to succeed is the purpose of the services conversation at IEP meetings. It's also what we do as parents every day.

Transition Plans

An important part of a student success plan is to prepare for life after high school. Life after high school is multifaceted; it includes personal, professional, and academic goals. This topic is covered in more detail in Chapter 5. As many of us likely experienced ourselves, postsecondary goals and plans change over time. In some ways, all adults are still figuring out this life-after-high-school thing. The other day, I was talking to a former student. This young man had an IEP in high school. He is now about to graduate college and is considering his next steps. He's not sure what's next for him—work, travel, or graduate school. He's also not completely sure what comes after any of those options.

"That's okay," I assured him. "I still don't know what I want to be when I grow up either."

This student, his family, and his teachers started thinking about life after high school long before his senior year. These conversations mattered. They led him to an undergraduate program where he was successful and happy. Now he's ready for his next transition, and although there isn't an IEP to help him through that process, he and his family are using the same strategies and conversations to also help him find the right fit for what is next.

According to IDEA, all students must have a transition plan included in their IEP once they turn 16 years old. Further, students must be an active part of their transition planning. I recommend, to the greatest extent possible, having students lead at least this part of the IEP. Often our ideas about a young person's postsecondary plans are colored by our personal experiences or worries and not the student's own interests. When we invite students to take the lead on talking through their hopes and postsecondary plans, we are often surprised by the direction and depth of their dreams. We can then work together to help young people take steps to prepare for career paths that truly interest them, recognizing that, just like with adults, sometimes these interests shift over time. The transition plan includes specific goals and supports for students related to their postsecondary aspirations. These may include vocational and job goals, academic goals, and independent living goals (if relevant). As with the other goals and services in an IEP, these are reviewed and revised annually.

Transition plans ask about how the student, school, and family will support students as they work toward their transition goals. For example, if a student is interested in programming, she might take a coding class, the school might help her find an internship in technology, and the family might offer to take her on a college visit to explore computer science majors. Or, if a student is working on independent living goals, he might commit to learning how to do his own laundry, the school might facilitate work experience at a local retail store, and the family might offer to help him set up his own bank account. IEPs should be highly relevant to our students' lived experiences. The transition plan, even if it changes annually (and even if those changes are significant), should always align with goals and interests that matter to the student. You'll notice, I said "goals" and "interests," not "abilities." I find that it's most helpful to start with big dreams. What do students want to accomplish? What do they see themselves doing? Once we have a dream, we can plan backward. We can meet with people in the desired profession. We can outline skills and training and start chipping away. We can have frank conversations with young people to explain that this may be a long and challenging path, and then we can affirm that we're here for them. If the proposed plan ends up not being a good fit, we can go from there and develop a new plan.

Meeting Summary and Signatures

At the close of the IEP, everyone should be clear on next steps and primary outcomes from the meeting. If services are changing, everyone should know when new services are beginning or current services are ending. Has the team agreed to a new behavior plan? If so, everyone should know when that plan is starting and who is preparing any needed materials for that plan (e.g., a behavior chart). If your child is present, clearly explain when and how things are changing in their school day. If your child is not present, you'll want to accurately and thoughtfully explain and prepare them for any changes. If this summary and timeline isn't clear at the end of the meeting, pause the meeting and ask for an overview of next steps. You can also ask who you should follow up with if you have questions about services or anything else in the IEP. Often this is your child's IEP *case manager*. A case manager is assigned once your child has an IEP. This person is usually a teacher or service provider in your child's school. The case manager is responsible for coordinating services, tracking progress toward goals, and making sure accommodations and modifications are provided as outlined in the IEP.

IDEA does not require parent or guardian signatures to formalize the IEP. However, some states have created their own policies for parents/guardians to sign off on implementing the IEP. To find out whether your state requires signatures, check your state department of education webpage. Although not required by federal law, many IEP teams will ask everyone who participates in an IEP meeting to sign a "record of participants." This often happens during introductions at the beginning of the meeting, but it can also happen at the end as a more final step. If you do not agree with the IEP, you can indicate your exceptions in writing (The Wrightslaw Way, 2010). If you have concerns or disagree with anything in the IEP meeting, I strongly recommend voicing those concerns during the meeting. Often these issues can be resolved during the meeting. I also know that often parents' emotions are charged during these meetings, and this clouds our thinking. As a writer and an introvert, I am always more comfortable taking home the issues I am working on, thinking through them, and then responding with more thoughtfulness later. However, in this case, it is often more effective not to wait. If your concerns cannot be resolved during the meeting, then you can (and should) follow up with a more formal letter outlining your concerns. Depending on the nature of your concerns, an additional IEP meeting may be needed for you and the team to come to a consensus on the best plan for your child.

What About Private Schools?

Private schools are not bound to exactly the same state and federal policies around special education that public schools are. Given this, private schools have a wide range of approaches toward supporting students who learn differently. Some private schools do not serve children with disabilities at all or are not equipped to serve children with moderate to profound disabilities. Some private schools have staff that are specifically trained in special education and able to honor your IEP. Still other private schools specialize in educating children who learn differently. As you are considering the best school option for your child, see Figure 12 for some questions to ask when meeting with administrators, counselors, and teachers at a prospective private school.

Questions to Ask Staff When Exploring a Private School

› Does your school serve children with disabilities, including children with moderate to profound disabilities?
› How familiar are you with [children on the autism spectrum, children who are medically fragile, children with learning disabilities]?
› How successful have other children with disabilities been at your school?
› Could you connect me with another family in your school community whose child also has disabilities?
› What is your school's philosophy on inclusion for children with disabilities?
› Where could my child get extra support at your school? Do you have a resource room? Do you have staff with a background in special education?
› My child has an IEP or 504 plan. Will you be willing and able to honor their IEP or 504? [For example, my child needs exams read aloud to them/needs a safe place in the school to calm down/requires a paraprofessional.]
› Is your building accessible for a child who uses a wheelchair?
› Do you have a speech, OT, or adaptive PE teacher on staff?
› Is there someone who will help my child take their medication every day?
› What is your school's philosophy toward discipline?
› May we observe a class?
› Could my child visit a class for the day?

Figure 12. Questions for private schools.

Services Plan

If your child has an IEP and will be attending a private school, know your rights. IEPs are legally binding under IDEA for children in public schools. Private schools do not have these same rules. That said, in addition to gathering information, families whose children attend private schools may also pursue an *Individual Service Plan.* You may hear this referred to as an ISP or services plan. Formal ISPs are written by the *local educational agency* (LEA), not the private school. To find out who your LEA is, you'll typically want to work with the school district where your child would attend public school. However, interpretations of LEA vary from place to place, and depending on where you live, your LEA may be a regional or state group.

ISPs do not entitle students to free and appropriate public education (FAPE). Because you are choosing a private school instead of a public school, it makes sense that FAPE isn't covered in an ISP. Instead, an ISP will translate the related service(s) your child would receive in public schools to *equitable services*, which the LEA will make available to your child. IDEA does require that some funding be allocated to equitable services for students with disabilities who attend private schools; however, this funding is limited and less protected than the funding for students in public schools. Further, the private school is not obligated to deliver these equitable services. This means that often if your child needs a service, such as speech or occupational therapy, you will likely need to provide your own transportation to the public school in your home district to receive these services.

As you are mapping out a services plan for your child at a potential private school, you will want to explore what accommodations and supports will be available in your child's new school. Although private schools are not obligated to, they can implement accommodations, such as extended time on exams or assignments, testing in a private setting, and chunking larger assignments. Engage the teachers and administrators in these conversations before you enroll, so that you and your child are fully aware of what supports will and will not be available.

With this information, you can make a well-informed choice about the best school for your child. It may be that the full range of services in public school makes the most sense, or it could be that the particularities of a private school are a better fit for your child. Keep in mind that children's needs change over time. The best fit in elementary school may not be as perfect a fit in middle school.

Don't Go It Alone

I want to close this chapter with two big takeaways. First, IEP meetings are emotionally taxing. Many of the parents I talked to during the writing of this book shared stories of crying in their cars before or after these meetings. I personally remember, shortly after one IEP meeting, showing up at my friend Beth's office and weeping. When she asked what was wrong, I said I wasn't sure. The truth was that I didn't know how to articulate the huge range of emotions I was feeling.

In talking to another friend whose child is also now grown, we shook our heads and said "the IEP years" were the hardest. We both said we wished we had talked more openly to our friends and other parents about all of these feelings and how hard the process was. Instead we chose to journey alone as an immediate family island in a sea of stress. Looking back, we could both see that was a mistake. Don't go it alone. Reach out. Schedule a lunch with a friend. Find a community with other families of children who learn differently. If the IEP brings up strong emotions for you, know that this is perfectly normal. As a parent and a human being, you may find that the IEP tends to strike a chord with the things you care most deeply about.

I believe in the adage that knowledge is power; having an idea of what to expect during an IEP hopefully helps make these difficult meetings more manageable. Use the information in this chapter to understand the different pieces of the IEP. Use it as a springboard for questions to ask. And please use it as an invitation to pause the meeting anytime you need more clarity or to shift the conversation to a strengths-based dialogue. Trust your instincts. You know your child better than anyone else in the room, and that perspective is invaluable. In Part II, I'll talk through how you can use that knowledge and passion to advocate with love.

Part II

Advocating With Love

Advocating with love means finding countless ways to tell our children:

›   I see you.
›   I will keep you safe.
›   I value your perspective.
›   I believe in you.
›   I am cheering for you.
›   I will make sure you are included.
›   You matter to me.
›   You belong.
›   We are in this journey together.

These statements are not based on your achievements or mistakes. *You are loved simply for being who you are.*

Chapter 4

Family Advocacy

Family advocacy[14] is a delicate dance between knowing when to step in and intervene and when to let your child navigate challenges on their own. This dance often gets more complicated as our children grow. During your child's school life there will likely be times when you need to step in and fill in the gaps between what is happening in the school environment and what your child needs. Cooperative relationships between families and schools can lead to excellent and creative support plans that work for kids. I've found that usually everyone involved, from the school team to the family team, wants what is best for your child[15]. That doesn't mean that everyone sees things the same way. Often we have to come together, sit around a table, fill in some gaps, and work out a new plan. You have important information that the school may be missing about your child's needs, experiences, and concerns. This knowledge is invaluable; remember, no one knows your child better than you. In this chapter, I'll give you an overview of family advocacy, focusing on how we talk about and facilitate conversations around our children's abilities, disabilities, learning needs, and behavior concerns. In the next chapter, we'll talk about translating these skills to teach our children self-advocacy.

---

14 Rather than the more common terms *parent advocacy* or *parent advocate*, I use *family advocacy* and *family advocate* to be inclusive of other guardians, grandparents, uncles, and aunts who may be raising children.

15 Of course, there are exceptions. In cases of discrimination and injustice, you may need to take a more pointed approach, including invoking your due process rights.

Family advocacy is about making sure that your child is seen, understood, and appropriately taken care of. Disability and/or learning differences often make the need for advocacy more pronounced. However, disability is only one part of a child's identity. There are other reasons your child may need you to step in and advocate on their behalf. Other cultural identity markers (e.g., religion, sexual orientation, culture), social-emotional needs or personality traits (e.g., introvert, anxiety, highly sensitive), or life experiences (e.g., health issues, trauma, or bullying) can all necessitate the wisdom of a caring family advocate. Even without the complications of disability, being a young person is hard. Family advocates and great teachers save our children again and again.

There are many times when we have to step in and intervene on behalf of our children. Family advocacy can be both proactive and reactive. When we can anticipate those tough moments in advance, often proactive advocacy can prevent a lot of heartache and confusion later on.

Each school year, I meet with our children's teachers at the beginning or in advance of the school year. I tend to frame this first conversation around our children's strengths, building relationships, and sharing essential information that I think will help their teachers meet my children where they are. When our son started middle school, his social studies teacher beat me to this meeting by sending home an assignment the first day of class asking families what they would like her to know about the children entering her class. As both a parent and a writer, I loved this opportunity and responded with the following letter.

Letter to My Son's Middle School Teacher

Dear Teacher,

On Thursday we dropped off a wide-eyed, leggy adolescent who shot up over the summer and now stands eye level to me. He wore cool jeans and a nervous grin. We watched him walk into the large middle school of 50-minute classes, algebra, and locker rooms.

Under your care, he will learn to survive a school day without soccer breaks at recess. He will learn to write things down in his planner. He will learn to play scales on the clarinet. He will learn to balance equations. He will learn to think critically about the things he reads and hears.

I hope he doesn't learn to think of school as a game about points. And I hope that you take the time to teach him that often the most important things we learn aren't ever tested on an exam.

He will learn to navigate friendships, romantic relationships, and peer pressure. Although we have talked to him about these things, I know there are critical moments when these conversations will need to occur again. Please be there for him when he has questions.

He will change in the 3 years he spends in middle school. He will—although I can't believe it—grow even taller. His voice will lower. He will learn he isn't the best at everything. He will learn disappointment. Sometimes when he learns these difficult lessons, you will be there. You will be the one who gets to him first. I hope you put your arm around him and remind him he is still an important and wonderful person.

While he is learning all of these things, I will worry and fret. I will feel the loss of Superman pajamas and toy cars. Yet, I will also remark at the young man my son is becoming. And I will breathe a sigh of relief each day when he slides onto the school bus and texts me (texts me!), "Hey Mom, I had a great day at school. I love you."

Appreciatively,
Jaxon's Mom

Strengths-Based Language

Our children are children. They are compassionate, creative, and idiosyncratic. They are interested in dinosaurs, trains, and sharks. They enjoy soccer, video games, and drawing. Sometimes people in our children's lives don't know how to talk about our children. Often this is because they don't know how to talk about disability. If the way someone is speaking about your child doesn't feel right, step in and gently correct. In recent years, there has been some debate among family advocates and people with disabilities as to whether "people-first language" or "identity-first language" is the best approach for talking about disabilities. I'll give you some background on both positions and then offer my own guidance on taking a "both/and" approach that puts children first while also valuing their complex identities as vibrant and interesting young people.

Both "people first" and "identity first" frameworks ask us to carefully consider how we talk about others in the disability community. This care for language, identity, and labels is a relatively new and highly needed practice. In fact, a handful of years ago I toured a brand-new school before it opened and saw that it had an "MR room." MR stood for "mentally retarded," a highly outdated and offensive term. I spoke up about how outrageous, offensive, and potentially illegal this kind of language was. I was subsequently assured the room would be renamed before the school opened—and it was. How we talk about people matters. Both people- and identity-first language demand a more thoughtful approach to how we speak about people with disabilities.

People-first language is a commitment to put a person before their disability. For example, instead of saying "a disabled person," you would say "a person with disabilities." This difference is more than just a semantic choice. Knowing that language shapes perception, people-first language proponents want to be sure that children's human identities are foregrounded before their disabilities. People-first language is an intentional and humanizing decision to see our children as children first.

The American Speech-Language-Hearing Association (ASHA) described the difference as a matter of possession versus identity (Folkins, 1992), and this is where identity-first language advocates step in. *Identity-first language* is a commitment to put the identities that a person values first. These identities may include a person's disability or membership in a specific culture, including disability culture. Let me give you an example and then a chart, so we can think through this together.

In graduate school, I had the good fortune of studying at San Francisco State University (SFSU), which has an excellent special education department, coupled with a strong institutional commitment to inclusion and accessibility. Although I haven't worked with many deaf students as a teacher[16], while studying at SFSU I had many Deaf classmates (capital D). My peers taught me about the Deaf community. Many members of the Deaf community choose to lead with their deaf identity, as they believe belonging to this cultural group is essential to who they are. For them, the capital "D" refers to culture, whereas a lowercase "d" refers to disability.

Members of the Blind community sometimes use similar language, and in recent years members of the autism community have also adopted this approach. For example, while writing this book, I met with several

---

16 Thus far in my career in education, I have only had a few deaf students. One student who stands out took a course I taught on radio storytelling. She challenged me to think differently about accessibility in the classroom, in the community, and certainly in radio. I am a better educator for having known her.

parents who self-identified as an "autism mom" or "autism dad." This surprised me, and so I explored this identification with some parents who were using the term. They chose this label to proudly identify with their children and also with the autism community. When I visited with a mother about leading with her child's identity in this way, she shared, "It [is] a way of expressing community and a common understanding of the fears, caution, and extra preparation that come along with caring for our children." We all have many identities. Although someone may be an "autism dad," he could also be an "adoptive dad," a "softball dad," a "room parent," and a "tired dad," all at the same time.

There is legislation to support more inclusive language. On October 5, 2010, President Barack Obama signed "Rosa's Law" (Pub. Law 111-256) into federal law. This law removed the terms *mental retardation* and *mentally retarded* from federal health, education, and labor policy and replaced them with people-first language, such as *individual with an intellectual disability* and *intellectual disability* (Spread the Word, 2019). I brought up this legislation when touring the school with the "MR room." As of July 2013, all 50 states passed their own similar bills requiring more inclusive language.

Whether you lead with the disability identity or the personal identity, speak from a place of love and high expectations and always honor the personal preference of the individual to whom you are referring. I've found that most people are very receptive to a gentle correction, conversation, or additional information about how to speak about disability, people with disabilities, or disability identities.

Although I've long used people-first language, working on this project and visiting with more children and families who proudly identify with the disability community has led me to a new perspective on how we talk about disability. *Strengths-based language* merges person-first and identity-first language. It's a strengths-based approach that honors children's complex identities and centers on their personal preferences. Figure 13 is a chart to help explain to your personal and school communities how to use strengths-based language.

For more information on reframing disability and the ways individuals with disabilities are proudly claiming disability identities, see the discussion on neurodiversity in Chapter 7. The language we use to talk about our children, families, and fellow human beings should be affirming and humanizing. If you don't know how someone (especially your child) prefers to identify, ask that person! If the way someone is speaking about you

Strengths-based language affirms the identities that children want to lead with. These language choices recognize that children are complex people with many identities, sometimes including a disability identity. Guiding principles of strengths-based language include

> › humanizing the way we talk about people, their identities, and the services or supports they use; and
> › honoring that children (and their families) offer the best guidance on what identities they want to be referred by.

Strengths-based language is informed by people-first language, identity-first language, and culturally responsive classroom practices.

Q: When referring to someone with a disability, how should I start the conversation?

A: Start with the person's strengths, identity, and culture!

Do Say	Don't Say
A child's name, preferred pronouns, or identity as a child, person, or student	Weakness or limitations in place of a child's identity
What a student *can* do (e.g., "Wow, this student [insert strengths and compliments].")	What a student *can't* do (e.g., "Wow, this student [insert limitations and disabilities].")

Q: What if I need to talk about disability or challenges?

A: Put the preferred personal/identity descriptor first. Does the child want to lead with their autism or Deaf identity? If so, honor their preferences. When in doubt, names are always a good place to start. Are you speaking more generally? Maybe you are talking about students, athletes, or children. If so, lead with that.

Do Say	Don't Say
A student/child/person with disabilities	Disabled student/child/person
A student/child/person who has Down syndrome	Down syndrome student/child/person
A student/child/person who learns differently	Learning disabled student/child/person
A student/child/person who has a brain injury	A brain-damaged student/child/person

Figure 13. Strengths-based language.

Q: What if I am talking about services?

A: We receive services, but we are not our services. Whenever possible, explain how a student uses these services and talk about accessibility, not limitation.

Do Say	Don't Say
Accessible school/classroom/playground	Handicapped school/classroom/playground
A student/child/person who uses a wheelchair, walker, or other assistive technology	A student/child/person who is confined or tethered to a wheelchair, walker, or assistive technology
A student/child/person who communicates with assistive technology	A nonverbal or mute student/child/person
A student/child/person who receives special education services	A special education student/child/person

Q: What if I don't know how a child identifies?

A: Ask! If the child isn't able to tell you their preferences, ask their family. Respect the answers that you learn.

Figure 13. Continued.

or your child doesn't feel right, speak up. You are welcome to offer Figure 13 as a reference. If you are in a conversation and unable to ask the person being referenced how they would like to be named, I recommend using people-first language and then respectfully asking at your first opportunity.

The Barber Shop Story

I have a professor friend who does research on *community-based pedagogical spaces*. This means he is interested in the kind of learning and teaching that happens in community spaces, such as parks and churches. When he first told me about his work, I was a bit surprised that one of his primary research sites was the barber shop. This means that (1) I didn't grow up in the Black community, and (2) I hadn't paid enough attention to the conversations happening at barber shops and salons. Then, I started writing this book.

Joan, the wonderful woman who cuts my hair, is a mother of eight. Her young son is an avid reader who is also on the autism spectrum. She and her family have tried different classroom settings for him throughout his early elementary years, and he's made great progress. Around the time I signed the contract for this book, Joan's family was moving to a new school district. Joan was concerned about what services would be like in their new school. Knowing that I worked in education, she asked if I had any guidance on navigating the process at their new school. We talked about our children in a real way, from a place of love and worry. We talked about her family's rights, especially those around related services. This conversation forever shifted our hair-cutting sessions away from ordinary topics, such as the weather or dinner recipes, to more courageous choices, such as the complexities and joys of parenting children with disabilities.

As it happens, I had usually finished another chapter draft just as it was time to again get my hair trimmed. This meant that my touchpoints with Joan became a regular part of this writing project. As I thought about the best way to craft these chapters, she became yet another consistent parent voice in my head. Now, as soon as I sit down in her chair, she tells me all about her son's progress (we talk a lot about communication), recent goals (we talk a lot about pragmatics[17]), and the new services the public school is exploring (most recently a new classroom with more paraprofessional support). It has truly been a gift to hear about her son's progress, and I'm grateful she's let me be a listening ear during her family's advocacy journey at this new school. Consistent with my professor friend's work on community-based pedagogical spaces, this conversation about caring for kids who learn differently isn't just a classroom conversation; it's a community one. A huge part of advocacy relates to asking questions, reaching out for help, collecting guidance, and turning to the person next to you to say, "Hey, could I ask you about something?"

Continuum of Services

While I was working on titles for this book, two different parents advised me to "be very careful" with how and where I used the phrase *special education services*. They said that although their children receive many

---

17 Interpersonal communication, such as turn taking in speech and attending appropriately to nonverbals.

services, they don't think of their children as "special education students." They're absolutely right! Special education refers to a range of services that can be delivered in a range of settings depending on a child's needs and the infrastructure of a school or district. Special education is a not a place or an identity. This means someone cannot *go to* special education; instead a person might go to a resource room or receive services or supports from a learning specialist. Further, someone cannot *be* special education.

Poudre School District in Colorado has stopped calling these services *special education* altogether. Instead this district calls its range of services for students who learn differently *integrated services*. Likewise, the Florida Department of Education (2019) calls its program *Exceptional Student Education* (ESE), which includes both special education and gifted education services. Much of this advocacy chapter is about how language matters. How you and your school frame special education services communicates what these services do and don't mean as you put together support plans for your child.

Figure 14 explores what is known as the *continuum of services*. The continuum of services is typically presented from the most restrictive environment to the least restrictive environment (LRE), which is determined by the access a student has or does not have to the general student population. Understanding the continuum of services begins with this essential question: Where is your child learning?

Placement, including what LRE means for your child, should be fluid; just because a child is currently learning in one setting doesn't mean that setting will continue to be appropriate next semester or school year. Our goal is to make sure students are always learning in the least restrictive environment possible. What that means can (and should) shift over time. In Chapter 5, we'll talk more about ways to adjust setting through both mainstreaming and inclusion. These practices give us more flexibility in thinking about where and with whom children learn. Place, space, and access are important topics in our advocacy conversations.

Behavior Supports and Advocacy

Behavior is another important and frequent topic in advocacy conversations. Often our children's atypical behaviors instigate those advocacy, or gap-filling, conversations that I mentioned at the beginning of this chapter. Children who learn differently, experience school differently, or

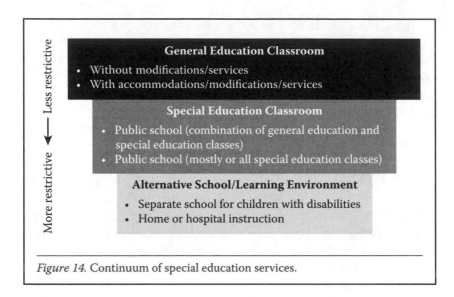

Figure 14. Continuum of special education services.

have disabilities frequently exhibit different behaviors than their peers. For this reason, behavior plans and behavior conversations are often part of an IEP or support plan. They are also often the reason you might get a call from school.

However, before we talk about strategies to either understand and/or remediate behavior or to advocate for your child's behavior needs, let's pause and remind ourselves that we are talking about children. *All* children sometimes exhibit behaviors that are inconsistent with what adults want to see. In working with children with disabilities on behavioral concerns, we want to be thoughtful about whether or not a behavior is developmentally typical for a child of that age and also whether it is linked to a child's disability. These distinctions sometimes help us with information about how to intervene. Some behaviors are perfectly normal as children learn and grow. I recently heard a colleague and family therapist remind a large group of parents that if a 3-year-old throws a temper tantrum, that's not only *not* a problem, but it is also developmentally normal. If children are throwing 12 temper tantrums a day, then it might be time to look into some different strategies to help them process their big feelings.

I like to think of this as the *They're Children Litmus Test* (TCLT). TCLT matters in behavioral remediation conversations. For example, the following are *not* behavior problems: feeling grumpy, frustrated, or tired; not wanting to play with a classmate; disagreeing (even with an adult);

making an honest mistake; or being clumsy. Let's remember that none of us (and I'm talking about adults here, too) are perfect. We all make mistakes, say the wrong thing, and accidently bump into someone in line. We don't always feel happy, nor are we always interested in engaging with the person across the room. Sometimes we need to take a minute or 10 to pause or even try again tomorrow. Sometimes we disagree with colleagues and friends. Disagreeing isn't a problem behavior; in fact, learning to disagree civilly and respectfully is a valuable and teachable skill. We (still talking about adults here) all sometimes accidentally knock over a water glass—gravity is real. Some of us are loud, naturally enthusiastic, and full of energy. Others of us are quiet, reserved, cautious, and perceptive. We don't want to quell these personality traits. Our wide range of emotions, behaviors, and personalities makes each of us unique. I say all of this to remind us to give each other, and certainly our children, more grace.

Often we can solve common behavioral challenges with creativity, meeting students where they are and giving young people more agency over their situations. Behaviors almost always happen for a reason. Agreeing or disagreeing with the reason doesn't do nearly as much good as identifying that reason and honoring that it matters to our children. Because behaviors tend to happen for a reason, giving an appropriate alternative that honors that reason is generally far more effective than simply telling young people to "stop." Finding the alternative that works for your child often takes a few attempts. If one strategy doesn't work, try another. Figure 15 offers a few common examples that have worked well in my classrooms and home.

It seems to me that sometimes we hold children to a higher behavior standard than we hold ourselves. Ironically, this seems even more true for students with disabilities whose behavior is very closely monitored. When talking to any child about behavior, use a calm, warm voice and tell children what you want to see as opposed to what you do not want to see. For example, "quiet feet" usually gets a better response than "stop stomping." Once you've vetted a behavior through the TCLT, tried giving grace and appropriate alternatives, and determined that you now need to address the behavior in a more systemized way, the next step is to collect data to better understand the behavior. If a behavior is inappropriate, avoidable, and becoming a pattern, then it may be time to think through some new targeted strategies. Behavior conversations require thoughtfulness and reflection. As we work on behavior supports, we want to make sure the

If you're seeing this . . .	You might try this . . .	You might say this . . .
Incessant foot or pen tapping	› Instruct the child to tap on the carpet or a knee instead of a hard surface. › Offer a fidget block or spinner.	"You have a lot of energy today. Let's try. . . ."
Missing homework	› Fill out a planner/agenda together. › Work together on homework before or after school and keep it in the classroom.	"Let's think together about how we can get your homework complete and turned in. I have some ideas. . . ."
Blurting out	› Have the child write in a notebook during class discussions. › Allow the child to whisper ideas to a paraprofessional. › Set up a "parking lot" where students can add ideas that the teacher will address later.	"I love that you have so much to say. Let's try something new to make sure we don't lose any of your ideas. . . ."
Throwing things	› Provide a drawing pad for doodling. › Offer a squishy ball to squeeze.	"We can't throw things in class, but there are other ways you can get your energy out. Let's try this. . . ."
Temper tantrums at transition time	› Proactive approaches: Use social stories (see Chapter 5) or give a gentle warning before a transition and let children set their own timer to signal when it is time to transition. › In-the-moment approaches: Acknowledge that the child is feeling something big and give options, such as moving to a quieter place.	"I can see that you are having some big feelings right now. Would you like a hug or to go somewhere quieter where we could talk about it together?"

Figure 15. Examples of appropriate behavior alternatives.

strategies we develop are meaningfully tailored to the child we are trying to help.

The ABCs of Behavior

Understanding behavior requires paying attention to the causes, context, and consequences of each incident. Behavior is usually a form of communication. As adults, it's our job to figure out what our children are trying to communicate. Figure 16 is a tool I designed that you can use for preliminary or informal behavior observations. This tool is based on the *antecedent, behavior, consequence* (ABC) approach. When working to understand what a child is trying to communicate or what is causing a behavior, be as specific as possible. The details you collect will help you identify patterns and salient variables that may be contributing to challenging behaviors. Use this tool to see things you might otherwise miss in the heat of a challenging behavior moment.

In the spirit of being honest and real, I want to pause here and acknowledge that it isn't always realistic to bring a behavior observation chart out to dinner. Some days just remembering to make sure everyone (including you) has eaten breakfast and brushed their teeth feels barely realistic. You don't always have the wherewithal to crouch down to your child's level, use a calm and compassionate voice, and carefully consider all of the context as to why this young person is screaming (again), why all of the chairs in the kitchen are upturned, and why a puddle of orange juice is pooling on the floor and now soaking into your socks. Maybe the school bus is turning onto your street at this moment, and your boss is calling on the phone. Maybe you couldn't sleep last night either. Part of being a parent is being human. This means you're not perfect; you aren't always as gracious and sensible as you want to be. I am literally writing a book on this stuff, and there are still times (many times) when I know I could have handled a situation with more wisdom and grace. Every day, the best we can do is the best we can do. Some days it is a gift to know that we get to try again tomorrow. And when we fall short of the way we wished we'd approached a stressful moment, we can be honest with ourselves and our children. We can say, "Hey, that was really hard for me. I didn't mean to raise my voice, and I am sorry. Let's work together on a better plan for me to help when you are feeling upset."

Incident 1		
Context: date, time, place, people present		
A	**Antecedent:** What happened immediately before the behavior?	Specific Notes:
B	**Behavior:** What was the behavior?	Specific Notes:
C	**Consequence:** What happened immediately after the behavior?	Specific Notes:
Incident 2		
Context: date, time, place, people present		
A	**Antecedent:** What happened immediately before the behavior?	Specific Notes:
B	**Behavior:** What was the behavior?	Specific Notes:
C	**Consequence:** What happened immediately after the behavior?	Specific Notes:
Incident 3		
Context: date, time, place, people present		
A	**Antecedent:** What happened immediately before the behavior?	Specific Notes:
B	**Behavior:** What was the behavior?	Specific Notes:
C	**Consequence:** What happened immediately after the behavior?	Specific Notes:

Figure 16. ABC informal behavior analysis tool.

Formal Behavior Processes and Tools

Schools have several tools to use within the IEP team to help children who struggle with behavior. Figure 17 offers a summary of *functional behavior assessment* (FBA), *behavior intervention plan* (BIP), and *positive behavioral interventions and supports* (PBIS). IEP teams use these tools to understand behavior and to help children make different choices to support their social and academic progress (von Ravensberg & Blakely, 2018). These processes will typically be discussed at your IEP meeting[18] and are

18 If your child is consistently struggling with behavior, the IEP team may move your meeting up in order to have this conversation sooner.

Tool	Acronym	What Is It?	What Does IDEA Say About It?
Functional behavior assessment	FBA	A process to identify and understand a specific behavior challenge, the purpose (function) of that behavior, and an intervention plan for positive replacement behaviors.	Included in disciplinary provisions since 1997, FBA has been suggested as a protection against suspension or expulsion as the primary response to challenging behavior and as a way to offer prevention-focused intervention. However, the wording is somewhat vague, and FBA is not yet required in IEPs.
Behavior intervention plan	BIP	A plan that outlines how the IEP team will help the child improve their behavior.	A BIP is required if behavior is indicated on the IEP as a challenge to academic success. A BIP is also usually written following or in conjunction with an FBA.
Positive behavioral interventions and supports	PBIS	A research-based, multitiered approach to social, emotional and behavior support, PBIS aims to improve the effectiveness of schools working with students on challenging behaviors.	FBA marked a significant shift in disciplinary philosophy for students with disabilities. As a result of this shift, the DOE set up a Technical Assistance Center on PBIS to report on research and evidence-based behavior interventions.

Figure 17. Formal behavioral tools.

required by IDEA if your child's behavior impedes their learning or the learning of others.

First, the team will want to identify the challenging behavior and understand as much as possible what is causing it. In educational speak, the team is trying to understand the function of the behavior. To understand behavior function, everyone involved must zoom in to look for details and zoom out to look for patterns. The five reasons children most often engage in behaviors are:

> to avoid (or get out of) something,
> to get something they are seeking (including attention),
> because it feels good,
> to express or cope with big, difficult emotions (e.g., insecurity, fear, embarrassment, or sadness), and
> because they didn't know the expectations.

Once the team understands (or thinks it understands) the function of a behavior, the next step is to make a plan to offer appropriate alternative behaviors to replace the challenging behavior. Given the many variables that contribute to behavior, support plans and resources must be closely monitored and frequently adjusted. The IEP or support team doesn't always figure it all out the first time; sometimes it still might not be completely right by the fifth time.

Understanding Ashton's Outbursts

Ashton was 7 years old when he joined my class in the middle of the year. Early one morning he, his mother, and his two younger siblings appeared in my classroom. They assumed I was expecting them. However, no one had told me I was getting a new student, and I was surprised to see them there. Ashton looked up at me, and I smiled at him. He flashed me a huge asymmetrical grin and took off racing across the room. Almost immediately he knocked off a large pile of papers sitting on my desk.

"Don't worry," his mother told me before I could address the fallen papers. "We don't let him wear those steel-toe shoes anymore. Too many people got hurt. He's in these soft Keds now, so everyone will be just fine."

I looked at the little boy who had now pulled out a huge tub of blocks and was building a tall, wobbly tower. *Steel-toe shoes! What does that mean?* I thought.

Ashton's mother gathered up the two younger siblings and said, "Bye, Ash. Listen to your teacher."

As his mother had alluded, Ashton was prone to violent outbursts. We tried many support strategies. Sometimes Ms. Pace, our paraprofessional, would take Ashton for a walk. Other times, I would take the rest of the class outside for an activity while Ashton calmed down. We made non-violence a classwide project. We read books and put on plays about being safe, kind, and a good friend. If I said "hands," all of my students (including Ashton) answered, "are not for hitting." We reinforced peaceful behavior with stickers and praise. These strategies helped, but not as much as I had hoped, and later I found out that they weren't helping for the reason I had thought.

After using FBA to better understand Ashton's behavior, we learned that Ashton's violent outbursts happened when he felt unsafe. It wasn't that he didn't understand the expectations. It wasn't that he needed attention or struggled with communication. If an exchange with a classmate felt volatile, if an activity made the room chaotic, or if we were in a new environment, Ashton's response was to act out. For Ashton, that looked like pushing and shoving. Once we realized this, our approach to Ashton changed. We focused on showing him that he was safe, wanted, and that he absolutely belonged in our classroom. These are powerful messages for all students, and for Ashton they were magic. Better understanding the causes of his behavior gave us more effective strategies for supporting him. Ashton spent 3 years in my classroom. In those years, he learned to read, write, solve math problems, and make friends. He was mainstreamed in early elementary classrooms with his general education peers. After the first few weeks, he was never referred to the office for behavior. With the right data, persistence, and creativity, parents and families can solve many behavior challenges, and the ones we can't solve (or haven't solved yet) we can approach with grace, dignity, and warmth.

Manifest Determination

Sometimes it is difficult to determine whether or not a challenging behavior is the product of a disability (which a child has little or no control over) or making a poor choice (which a child has control over). If the behavior is due to a disability or lack of needed services to support a disability, most educators believe it is unfair to punish a child, especially with consequences that remove the child from their educational environment (e.g., suspension or expulsion). This is why *manifest determination* was first introduced to IDEA in 1997. Manifest determination is a review process aimed at determining whether or not a behavior is a manifestation of a child's disability, a failure to implement the IEP, or a poor choice on the part of the child.

This is one of the most misunderstood sections of IDEA. If you've heard someone say that it is illegal to suspend a child with disabilities, that person is mistaken and probably citing a false interpretation of this legislative section. That said, there is plenty of research (Krezmien, Leone, & Achilles, 2006) to support that suspension is an ineffective behavioral remediation strategy for *any* child, and that students with disabilities are suspended at higher rates than their general education peers. However, manifest determination does not mean a school can't suspend a child with a disability; it means that there are times when a school must determine whether or not a behavior is a *manifestation* of the disability.

In the 2004 reauthorization of IDEA, manifest determination was simplified to include only two criteria. A manifest determination review must be conducted if:

> a student's removal from the educational environment due to behavior would constitute a change in placement, or
> a student is suspended from school for more than 10 consecutive days.

In either of these cases, a manifest determination review is warranted to understand whether the student's behavior was due to a disability or the school's failure to appropriately implement the child's IEP. If either of these criteria are met, the student's conduct must be determined to be a manifestation of the disability, and removal or suspension from an educational environment is considered inappropriate. A manifest determination must be conducted within 10 days of the behavior incident.

Manifest determination review is conducted by the IEP team. This team must include both the district or school local educational agency (LEA), who can commit district resources to the plan, and the parent/ guardian. Other team members may also be included, as appropriate. The team will review the IEP, the behavior incident, and the assigned consequences, and make a determination together. If the team determines that the behavior is the result of a disability or the failure of the school to implement the IEP, then the child's placement cannot be changed unless the team also determines that this is the best decision for the child's behavior plan. If an FBA and BIP do not already exist, both should be written as part of the manifest determination.

When working with serious behavior concerns, such as those that warrant a manifest determination, we use the same skills we use when working with smaller behavior concerns. We want to identify the function of the behavior, and then create support plans that will teach children safer and more appropriate behavior alternatives. Using love and high expectations in our approach to behavior means treating children with dignity while also giving them clarity and grace.

Critical Persons

Coach D saw our son at his best and his worst, and was unwavering in his support and love. Coach D watched Jaxon grow from a squirrely freshman who showed up late to practice or missed practice altogether to go play catch at the park, to a strong track star who ran on the district qualifying varsity relay team. Coach D was also instrumental to this growth. One year our son had an issue in school and wasn't able to finish the cross country season. Coach D told him, "I heard what happened. Keep running. We have track in the spring. And remember, I know you're a good person." That message meant the world to Jaxon and also to us.

Jaxon and the hundred plus other students in our school running programs stuck with Coach D, getting up at 6:00 a.m. for early morning practices and completing 8-mile runs on 100-degree days. Kids will do just about anything for a coach or teacher who believes in them. With some advocacy on our part, Jaxon was blessed to have Coach D for English his junior year and then to serve as his teaching assistant senior year . When Jaxon found his dream college program, Coach D wrote him an enthusiastic recommendation letter that helped him get in.

A few months after high school graduation, Jaxon ran his first marathon. We credit much of his success as both a runner and a student to Coach D, who is what one of my professors in graduate school called a *critical person*. A critical person can be anyone who sees children not only for all they are right now, but also for who they might become. Maybe it's a media center specialist who makes your child feel safe, a case manager who can redirect your daughter when she is upset, a coach who helps your son feel connected to a team, a counselor whose door is always open when your child needs a caring listener, or a paraprofessional who is always encouraging your teen. When you find that critical person, seek out as many ways as possible for that person to be part of your child's success plan. At one K–8 school I worked at, our lead custodian organized a leadership group for boys, giving them opportunities to serve our community and bringing in inspiring guest speakers who told these young men that they were the leaders our school needed. This custodian's initiative made an essential difference in how the boys in the program thought of themselves and their role in our communities.

A critical person can be the determining factor that helps a child reach their goals, feel included in school, and realize their potential. When you find one of these professionals who understands your child—who sees your child not just for who they are now, but also for who they might become—hold fast to this person. Invite this critical person to your IEP meetings. Find ways to schedule this person's support and compassion into your child's schedule. And remember, you can never thank these people enough. They are the love and high-expectation warriors at your children's schools.

Chapter 5

Raised on Love

Raised on love (ROL) is a term my husband and I came up with during the foster adoption process. It helped us make sense of some of the things we were seeing with our son, particularly the incredible power of love to help children heal and grow. When our son came to us, he was malnourished and small. He had recently broken his legs. He was just out of the casts and surgery. I took him to regular physical therapy appointments. We thought he would always have a "character walk." We were wrong. Within a year he was running in a youth track program and winning first-place ribbons. He is now 6'3" and runs marathons. Although calcium and physical therapy were helpful, we credit love as the primary reason he grew and excelled. *Thriving* is a term often used by adoptive families and social workers once children are placed in their forever homes. It sounds abstract, but there are concrete indicators of thriving, too. For example, in his first year in our family, Jaxon grew by six pant sizes.

While I was talking to Stephanie, one of my close friends, about this book, she said, "I hope your editors let you keep all of this talk about love." She said we don't talk much about love in education. She's right. I'm not sure we talk about love enough in parenting either. In schools, perhaps we think that love is too soft or personal for the professional and standardized space. Maybe when it comes to child raising, we take it for granted. The truth is, you can't raise (or work with) kids without love.

We will go tremendous lengths for the people we love. Love plus action is the most effective form of advocacy I've ever encountered. For our children, we will move to a new district. Normally quiet parents will demand a meeting with the principal. We will take a deep breath and intervene even when it is uncomfortable. We will stay up night after night worrying, and morning after morning letting our children know we believe in them and are in this together.

Wired for Inclusion

Never underestimate the inclusive potential of young children. I believe young children are wired for inclusion. Throughout my career in education, I have been consistently inspired by the ways in which young children are quick to make friends with peers who are different from them. This doesn't mean that young children don't see differences; it just means that these differences rarely impact who a child wants to color with, kick the ball with, play *Candyland* with, or build a huge tower out of multi-colored blocks with. It also doesn't impact who a child chooses to give a hug to or receive a hug from.

Will children ask questions about why their friends are different? Of course. Children ask questions about everything. Some of them haven't yet had a friend with physical disabilities or a friend who uses assistive technology. A simple answer is usually all it takes to satiate their curiosity. Giving your child that simple answer, such as "this helps them talk," "these help them walk," or "this helps their weaker eye grow stronger," is usually sufficient to get children back to the important business of playing, learning, and making friends. We could all learn a lot from young children.

Typically, I find that adults are far more worried about how their young children will do in diverse environments than children are. There are lots of reasons for this. For instance, many of us didn't have inclusive classrooms in our own childhoods. For many parents, our school-age contact with peers who had disabilities was limited or nonexistent. Thankfully, this is no longer the world children are growing up in or the schools that they attend. Although we still have a long way to go, we've also come a long way. Children with disabilities are increasingly included in our mainstream world, and our world is better for that inclusion and visibility.

Representation is a strong theme in this book; representation matters. What identities are featured and how they are portrayed have a profound impact on our worldview and perspective. Like other parents, I am encouraged by the inclusion of people with disabilities in recent advertisements

from major companies. In an interview in 2015, Target issued the following statement about the company's inclusive approach to advertising:

> At Target, our core beliefs of diversity and inclusivity are
> reflected in our advertising and in our business overall.
> We've included people with disabilities in our advertis-
> ing for more than 25 years and are humbled by the sup-
> port we've received recently. . . . We look forward to a day
> when diversity of all types in advertising is no longer a
> topic of discussion, but a way of life. (as cited in Heasley,
> 2015, para. 5)

In 2018, Gerber selected a baby with Down syndrome for the Gerber
baby of the year. In an article for the *Today* show, Katie Drisol, the founder
and president of a nonprofit committed to equal representation of individuals with disabilities in advertising and media, said, "We believe if brands
represent children with a disability, they are communicating their value to
our society. . . . Moves like this move us closer to a more inclusive world"
(Peters, 2018). I've found that this ideal, in which diversity is simply a way
of being, is most realized in our classrooms for very young children. I am
certain this is why these classrooms are among my favorite places to be.

Mainstreaming: Integrating Spaces in Schools

My first teaching position was in an early elementary classroom for
students with disabilities. This position taught me everything I know
about teaching. When we launched our program, I was teaching in what
is called a "self-contained" classroom. The idea was that all of my students'
learning would be "contained" inside this classroom. I had other ideas.
Learning should never be contained to the four walls of a classroom, and
groups of students should never be isolated from their broader peer group.
Therefore, I sought out every opportunity to make sure that my students
were included or mainstreamed with their peers in general education.
Mainstreaming is the practice of integrating a student with disabilities into
the general education classroom. I also wanted to be sure that the students
in the general education first-grade program were reciprocally included in
our classroom.

Thanks to some critical colleagues who partnered with me on this
endeavor, we adopted new approaches to managing our class rosters, we

said yes to huge integrated projects (like painting a mural or recording a CD together), and we took numerous field trips to learn outside of the classroom. These experiences made us better educators and better human beings, too. At the beginning of our second year, my two colleagues from the first-grade team and I launched an extended unit on marine ecology. The unit covered marine biology, ecology, and environmental sustainability. It included field trips to swamp lands and the San Francisco Bay. It culminated in the dedication of a student-designed mural on life in the bay. To teach content, my colleagues and I combined our three rosters, randomized them, and divided by three. We then taught specialized lessons and rotated students through our three rooms, similar to the way older students change classes in middle or high school.

Of course, there were challenges, but these challenges were not insurmountable. Some of my students needed to have a paraprofessional rotate with them. My teaching colleagues needed some training around my students' accommodations and modifications. Do you know who didn't need a lot of training? The students. They were thrilled. They loved changing classes like the middle school students and enjoyed learning with new friends. We taught extended units using this model for 2 years, and we never had any issues with bullying, exclusion, or safety concerns. All of the students learned, created work they were proud of, and made new friends.

I share this story in part to restore your faith in humanity. We simply don't hear enough stories of inclusion and friendship. That means we have to seek them out and live them. For me, visiting classrooms with young children has always restored my hope for the world. I also share this story to encourage more mainstreaming and inclusive practices in schools. Children learn best in inclusive environments. It's almost always the adults who are worried or reluctant. Look for ways to make sure your child is included with peers who do not receive special education services. If your school is not offering your child these opportunities, be bold and suggest them yourself. I know the classrooms and schools your children attend may not look like the one I just described. I know this because many of the classroom stories I share in this book are about partnership and expectations that have *never* been tried before. When we first proposed them, many of these ideas were met with doubt and even reluctance.

When you go into a meeting to advocate for a new mainstreaming opportunity, it helps to know that you may be suggesting or brainstorming something that no one has suggested or implemented before. Anticipate needing an honest brainstorm with the team about the supports your child will need in this new setting. Will your child need a paraprofessional to go with them? Will a paraprofessional need to visit the classroom ahead of time to become familiar with the space or staff working in that room? Have you asked your child which classrooms, classes, activities, or peers they might be interested in getting to know? Not sure where to begin with inclusion? Art, music, and PE can be great starting places.

Reverse Mainstreaming: A Sister School Story

Reverse mainstreaming is the practice of integrating students who do not receive special education services into classrooms or schools for students with disabilities. The previous example of dividing our rosters in three and rotating students through both my self-contained classroom and the general education classrooms included reverse mainstreaming. The general education students who rotated through my classroom were able to make new friends and experience a different environment.

Another example of reverse mainstreaming was a "sister school" project my class started when I was running a gifted education program for high school students. During my work in gifted education, it became clear very quickly that the students in our advanced programs almost never interacted with our students who had profound disabilities, and vice versa. This is not unusual in schools. Students with profound needs often receive most (or all) of their education in these separate spaces. This book is, in part, a call to help give you the advocacy tools to change this norm for your child and for all children. Over the past 15 years, I'm happy to report that I've met parents, teachers, and students who are building bridges to blur these boundaries in our schools. If your child isn't yet spending a lot of time with students who learn differently from how your child learns, advocate for opportunities to make new friends and experience different educational environments. This is exactly what happened with our sister school.

One Monday, a student and I were walking around our high school campus (I often had walking conferences with students). On this particular day, we walked to the far edge of campus and paused outside a small brick building just on the periphery of our school property. This building, which most of my colleagues, students, and even I hardly noticed, was home to a responsive K–12 school for students with profound disabilities, particularly students on the autism spectrum and students with behavioral and emotional disorders. My student and I looked at each other. The student smiled; she knew me well enough to know what I was thinking.

The next day, it was raining. The energy in my classroom was palpable, the sky was dark, and my students were restless for a new adventure. This seemed like the perfect moment to reach out to the responsive school. I picked up the phone and called. A kind secretary answered the phone. I introduced myself, shared that I had a small group of high school volunteers, and asked what their protocol was to train volunteers. Then the very kind woman laughed at me.

No one had ever called to volunteer there. Ever.

So we worked together to create a training protocol for my high school students. On our first day, my students and I walked down the street to the responsive school. None of us were sure what to expect. We met the secretary, signed in, and an administrator took us for a school tour. A few minutes into the tour, she got called to help a struggling student. We walked with her and saw a young man in distress. The administrator and a teacher were working patiently with him, but he was getting progressively more worked up. Suddenly he pushed over a chair and took off running out the front door and down the street.

My students looked to me.

I figured we were there to make new friends, learn, and be of service, so, I led my group to a nearby classroom. The teacher was a bit surprised to see a new group walking into his room. However, when I said we were there to help, he put us right to work. Within 20 minutes, my students were partnered up with new friends, playing science games on iPads, reading books, and working with the math manipulatives.

On the walk back to school my students had lots of questions. My favorite question was "Can we go back tomorrow?"

Over the next 2 years, we spent 1–2 afternoons a week at the responsive school. Sometimes my students struggled to understand what their new friends were saying. Sometimes my students struggled to explain a concept. Sometimes they had questions about specific modifications or assistive technology. Over the next 2 years, we learned a lot about both learning and friendship. One of my students said,

> I think everybody has an area where they might be considered 'having special needs' . . . I think it's incredible how changing an approach can change somebody's entire attitude toward an activity. There is a right method

for everyone, and it is all about having enough patience
and perseverance to find and use it.

I watched as my class fell in love with our sister school. During our
time there, we saw new students come to the responsive school, and we
also saw students exit the school and return to their traditional public
schools. In fact, one of my students got to support a student when she
transitioned back to our high school. These two young people were so
excited to go to the same school, have lunch together, and give each other
high fives in the hall.

I share this story for two reasons. First, I want to highlight that placement is fluid. We worked with students who needed the supports of our
sister school, and we also saw times when those supports were no longer
necessary and when students' needs could be appropriately (and better)
met in a less restrictive environment. Second, I cannot overstate the vital
role that inclusion plays in schools. When students with disabilities are
truly included in school communities, we all benefit from the lessons we
learn and the friendship we share.

One of my high school students who participated in this reverse mainstreaming project said, "in working with these students I discovered a part
[of our community] I hadn't known, and more surprisingly I discovered
myself."

As you are working with school professionals, I hope these stories give
you the confidence to ask about opportunities for mainstreaming, reverse
mainstreaming, and inclusion. If you have ideas for new partnerships,
please suggest them. Feel free to share our sister school story or any of the
other stories in this book that might help your child's success team think
more creatively about new inclusion opportunities.

Social Stories and Social Scripts

Social stories and *social scripts* help students have more comfort, confidence, and strategies for a variety of situations. They give students proactive and individualized directions for tackling social situations. Social
stories do so in narrative or story form, making children the protagonists
of their story. Social scripts help students with common dialogues, so that
they know what is appropriate to say in a given situation. Sometimes social
scripts and social stories are used synonymously. Rather than splitting

hairs there, I see both as important in helping children navigate new social situations, including services. Let's look at a couple of examples.

Social Stories

I use social stories before field trips and new activities. They are also terrific for daily routines. Social stories are written in first person and spell out expectations for navigating a specific situation or process. They can be illustrated with photographs of specific settings or behaviors. For example, if I were going to take Calvin, a child with intense social anxiety, to visit the library for the first time, I would probably use a social story to help him. To prepare the social story, I would go to the library ahead of time, speak with the media specialist, take photographs of the different spaces, and then use this information to put together a "going to the library" social story for Calvin. This story would begin with how we are getting to the library, how we enter the library, who we'll meet at the library, what kind of voices we use at the library, what will happen when we check out books, and how we will get home or back to school when we leave the library. Ideally, I would include pictures for each of these steps. Calvin and I would read this social story together several times *in advance* of our library visit. If he wanted, he could even bring the social story with him on our trip and point out steps as we do them together. The text of this social story might sound something like Figure 18.

If I were preparing this example for a young child, each line would be written on a new page, preferably with an accurate photograph illustrating the text. Older children might not need as many pictures; just the text and one or two pictures may be sufficient. Notice how I used simple, developmentally appropriate language. This story helps Calvin know what to expect in the social and physical environment. Social stories can also anticipate some of the stress points. For example, I knew taking the books away to scan them at checkout might be stressful for Calvin, so I wrote a sentence to let him know that this is part of the process and that he'll get his books right back. Social stories help demystify new situations, thereby decreasing anxiety and setting clear expectations for children.

Social Scripts

I use social scripts specifically to help children know what to say in different common situations. For example, I might write a social script for

---

Calvin Goes to the Library: A Social Story

The library is only a few blocks from our house.
On Saturdays, I can walk there with my mom.
I hold her hand when I cross the street.
The library is a big building with lots of books.
I have to be quiet when I go into the library.
One of the rules is to use a "whisper voice."
The person who works at the library is called a media specialist.
At our library, her name is Ms. Ann.
Ms. Ann will show us where the children's books are.
I can ask her to help me find books about trucks, dinosaurs, trains, or any-
   thing else I am interested in.
Mom and I can sit on the red and blue chairs or in the big purple bean bag
   and read together.
I get to choose three books to bring home with me.
Mom has a library card that we will give to the person at the front desk.
That person will take the library card and my books, but will give them right
   back.
Then we'll put the books in our backpack and walk home.
In 2 weeks, we'll bring our books back to the library, and I can choose three
   new ones to borrow.

Figure 18. Social story example.

---

buying a soda at a convenience store, asking to use the restroom, sharing information about accommodations, answering a question about disability or services, needing help with a math problem, etc. The following are a few examples:

> › I use a power chair to get around. Although I can't do stairs, my chair doesn't slow me down. I even play on a basketball league. Want to play basketball with me sometime?
> › My IEP says I can take my tests in the resource room. May I please work on my test there?
> › I've tried to solve this math problem, and I need some help. Would you help me with the next step?

Like social stories, social scripts lessen anxiety and give students strategies to navigate different social situations. Often, I'll practice social scripts with students through role-playing before they enter a new social situation.

Mental Contrasting

When raising and educating children, there is a lot of talk about goals. We ask our children what they want to be when they grow up and what they want to do after high school. We ask students what goals they are working on. We have them set homework goals and sports goals. For our children who receive special education services, we remind them about their IEP goals. Often we even set goals *for* our students. Clearly goals matter. However, many times we miss the most critical steps in helping our children set and achieve goals that matter to them. If all we do is ask students to tell us their goals, research suggests that young people actually become less likely to achieve these goals (Oettingen, 2014). And if we are the ones setting goals for our children without their investment or input, they're even less likely to be engaged in reaching them. We are all motivated to work on goals that matter to us. Teenagers are no exception to this rule; in fact, teenagers may have made this rule. If we want to help our children achieve at high levels, we have to ask them what they are interested in achieving. But we can't stop there.

What is the step we are missing? Many of us are not being real and proactive about the challenges or obstacles that stand between where a child is right now and where a child wants to be. This conversation can be the essential differentiator between having a plan to persist in the face of challenge and not having the strategies to problem solve when the going gets tough. Motivation psychologists call this *mental contrasting*, which involves visualizing both goals (wishes) and challenges (obstacles) to develop action plans that work (Oettingen et al., 2009). As you are setting goals with your child or teenager, I encourage you to use what Oettingen (2014), a motivational psychologist, called WOOP (wish, outcome, obstacle, plan).

Wish. Ask your child to share a wish. I often ask young people to share a short-term wish, a long-term wish, and a stretch wish (a wish that seems almost impossible). Note that working through WOOP takes time; you might not want to tackle three wishes in the same conversation. All of the wishes should be specific, realistic, and within your child's control. (That said, I encourage you to be quite liberal about what is possible.) For example, Jake, a 10th grader, might wish to pass geometry, appear on his local radio station, or make the basketball team. Although all of these might be challenging, they are within his control. If these goals matter to your child, these are great wishes to work on. However, if Jake hoped to make someone fall in love with him, be given a million dollars, or grow to 6'5", these goals are outside of what he can control. If your child has these kinds of wishes, no amount of work can make them come true, so you'll want to help your child identify some different goals to work toward.

Outcome. Once your child has identified a wish, the next step is to describe the outcome. What will it look like and feel to like when that wish comes true and the goal is met? This is a fun question; enjoy exploring it together.

Obstacle. Next, you need to have an honest conversation about the obstacles standing between where your child is right now and what it will take to make the wish come true. Be specific. Model an open conversation about obstacles by working through this process alongside your child.

Plan. Finally, for each obstacle your child identifies, develop a plan to overcome that obstacle. For example, if your daughter's goal is passing algebra, she might say an obstacle is learning how to use her graphing calculator. As a family you can brainstorm a plan to get her more support with using a graphing calculator: Maybe there is a math tutor, older student, or YouTube channel that can help. This way, when her math teacher asks the class to practice problems on their graphing calculators, your daughter already has some practice figuring this part out. Every obstacle requires its own plan. Together these plans provide clear and targeted direction for making our wishes come true.

Oettingen and colleagues' (2009) research on mental contrasting is exciting and provides a terrific model for working with older students. Teenagers often have lots of wishes and goals, and this practice can give them a problem-solving model that allows them agency over making their own wishes come true. As we consider the other topics in this chapter, remember the importance of helping our children contrast where they are now with where they want to be, and encouraging them to believe that with strategies and effort they can persist through the challenges in between.

Self-Advocacy

Self-advocacy is the ability to make sure one's needs are understood and met. This can look like speaking up, speaking out, stepping in, and educating others. Although there are some common skills and mindsets we can teach to help young people practice self-advocacy, the way each person advocates is necessarily contextualized by individual personalities, identities, and communication styles. Self-advocacy is an essential skill for everyone to develop. For people with disabilities, it can be the key to getting the services, accommodations, and supports needed to be successful. I believe that young children should start working on self-advocacy skills early. Like any skill, the more that kids practice self-advocacy, the more effective they become at it. In thinking about how to work with children on self-advocacy, I work on three key areas: self-concept, self-efficacy, and communication. See Figure 19 for more information on this framework.

Self-advocacy goals can be positive additions to IEPs. With older students, I often see goals that ask students to educate their teachers about their disability and accommodations. This is a great practice for when and if students work with disability services in college or careers. However, let's not forget that there is also a lot we can do around self-advocacy that isn't disability-specific. Two such skills I like to focus on are (1) developing an emotional vocabulary (see the following section) and (2) practicing strategies for conflict management. Both of these are terrific assets to self-advocacy. As parents and teachers, we are often too quick to jump in to help solve our children's problems. I get it. We love our kids, and when we see something isn't going well, we want to fix it. Here's the thing though: Our children need to know that we believe they can solve problems on their own. In fact, letting young people navigate some of their own challenges is an act of love and high expectations. Solving problems requires self-concept, self-efficacy, and communication (see Figure 19). We want to help children recognize and appreciate their strengths and identities. We want them to know that they can persist through challenges, which, of course, means having some challenges to practice with. Finally, they need to be able to effectively share their perspective with others. Social scripts, discussed earlier in this chapter, may also be a helpful support for communicating needs.

Inviting students to participate and even lead parts of their IEP meetings can be an excellent practice in self-advocacy. I once worked with a colleague who frequently invited her high school students, including those with profound disabilities, to lead their IEP meetings. She worked with her students ahead of time on preparing PowerPoints to present to the IEP team, thinking about their strengths, and reporting on their own progress toward their IEP goals. I loved attending these student-led IEP meetings and hearing the ways students thought of themselves as learners and how they best thought adults could support them in achieving their goals. I would go so far as to say that students have the most important perspec-

A Framework to Help Students Develop Self-Advocacy Skills		
	Definition	**Guiding Questions**
Self-concept	Understanding your strengths and identities, and being able to frame these positively and accurately.	Who are you? What are your strengths? What makes you unique and special?
Self-efficacy	A belief that you can persist through challenges.	What strategies can you use when things aren't going the way you would like?
Communication	Being able to effectively share your perspective with others.	How will you share this message? How can you get someone to listen to you?
Self-advocacy	The ability to make sure your needs are understood and met.	What do you need in this situation? How can you make sure your needs are met?

Figure 19. Understanding self-advocacy.

tive on their education. Giving young people the tools to be heard when they share their perspectives can lead to more effective success plans in school and life, and deeper understanding for everyone.

Emotional Vocabulary

For children, a big part of making sure their needs are met is being able to describe how they are feeling in a situation. Having a robust emotional vocabulary can make communicating feelings a lot more effective. If you ask children how they are feeling, they are likely to tell you that they feel happy, sad, or scared. When a child tells me this, I ask, "What kind of happy, sad, or scared?" and then we talk about the different kinds or layers of emotions we have (see Figure 20).

There are many wonderful activities you can plan around emotional vocabulary with your child. You can draw emotions, share stories about different times you've experienced these emotions, play charades with

What Kind of Happy, Sad, or Scared?		
Happy	› Excited › Joyous › Silly › Elated	› Proud › Confident › Peaceful › Glad
Sad	› Worried › Homesick › Lonely › Frustrated	› Disappointed › Gloomy › Low › Weary
Scared	› Nervous › Insecure › Sick › Unsafe	› Concerned › Alarmed › Panicked › Terrified

Figure 20. Developing an emotional vocabulary.

emotions, challenge each other to come up with the longest possible list of emotions, or find an emoji for different emotional vocabulary words. Being able to name their feelings gives children agency. Understanding that there are a range and depth of emotions helps children more effectively explain what they are feeling and what they need.

As children develop emotional vocabularies, be careful not to dismiss their emotional assessments. If a child tells you she is feeling alarmed, don't tell her she isn't or shouldn't feel alarmed. Instead ask her why she is feeling alarmed. Ask her how you can help ease her concerns. Her feeling belongs to her, and only she knows how she is feeling. Likewise, if a child is crying, telling him not to cry isn't going to do much to help the situation. Instead, affirm that the child's emotional experience is his own. Ask questions about why he is feeling that way and what he needs in the situation. Recognizing that everyone has a wide range of feelings, and honoring those emotions as valid, is an empowering practice you can start working on even with very young children.

Another note to remember in working with feelings is that emotions are often contagious. If you approach a heated situation with anger or panic, you'll likely escalate the emotional temperature. However, if you approach a heated situation with calm and compassion, you can often deescalate the temperature by bringing some new emotions to the situation. In fact, often when I enter a situation in which voices are raised, I'll intentionally speak in a very quiet voice. This frequently leads to everyone quieting their voices and taking a deep breath. Working with big feelings or challenging behaviors is tough. The more you can be intentional in your choices and in tune with your own feelings, the more you'll be able to support your children when they need this extra support.

Life After High School

I was walking downtown with a colleague from another academic department. She asked what projects I was working on. I had just started writing this book.

"Could I tell you about an idea I have for a book?" I asked.

"Absolutely."

"Okay. Tell me if you think this idea would be useful." I started with the story of Ann reaching out on Facebook. I told my colleague that I wanted to write a book to help families navigate the special education process with love and high expectations. I could feel myself getting more animated as I shared the idea. I told her what my husband, Chris, had said—that if it wasn't for my degree in special education and background experiences in the classroom, he doesn't think we would have had any idea about how to advocate for our son.

We were almost back to campus, and I noticed that we had slowed down. I told her, "There are a lot of books out there on specific disabilities and a lot of books out there on how professionals can work with families. This isn't that book. I think for the most part what families navigate when supporting children who learn differently isn't dependent on the specific disability. What I want is to give families a book they can use to navigate inclusion, high expectations, processes, services, etc. What do you think?"

"Hell yes!" Her enthusiasm took me by surprise. She laughed and explained. "As the mother to a son with autism, I often have no idea about, well, most of this. And I have a Ph.D.! It seems like I should be able to figure this out. I want to know when it is okay for me to throw a fit. What are our rights as a family? And, what in the world are we going to do after high school?"

I hadn't known about my colleague's son and was touched that she was willing to share her story. I asked her a few questions about where her son was in school and what his experiences had been like. The family's biggest worry right now was what he was going to do after high school. I offered to connect her to some local resources. We stood together on the sidewalk two blocks away from her office on a hot August day, swapping stories about our children. She told me about her son's goals and her fears. Later, I went home and opened my computer. First, I sent her some information about vocational rehabilitation (see Figure 21 on p. 109), and then I opened the file for this manuscript, typing with a heightened resolve to see it through. . . .

Because I promised to tell it to you straight, I feel like I have to let you know that there is a little more to this story. After this conversation, I did sit down to work on the book. I did have heightened resolve to see it through. However, I also felt so lucky that my family had already found the *perfect* postsecondary program for our son. And then a couple months later, it turned out it wasn't a perfect fit.

Remember this feeling? You worry when your child starts a new school or program. You fret. You don't know if you made the right choice, and then, to your surprise, it starts off fine. Your child (whether young or grown) experiences one success and then another. You breathe a sigh of relief—and then there's a big setback. It shakes you to your core and validates all of those worries. Sometimes before you recover, there's another setback. My family was there—again.

I reminded myself that our family would overcome this challenge. We'd work it out together. We'd set up a new plan. I had faith. We had done this before, many times. I told myself that soon we'd find our way, soon we would experience another success, and I would breathe a more cautious sigh of hope. It was then that I realized this process will repeat ad nauseum. I knew that the worrying, loving, and celebrating were lifelong parts of parenting, but I hadn't considered that the advocacy, navigating, and support planning were, too.

While our children are in high school, there is a lot we can put in place to help make their postsecondary transitions smoother. However, making sure our (grown) children's needs continue to be met also requires ongoing supports and continued problem solving that we'll work through together. Figure 21 is a chart of helpful considerations as you are planning for or navigating your child's postsecondary journey.

Remember, raising children isn't a solo activity. Navigating school is a journey, and navigating life is an even bigger journey! Ask questions and seek recommendations from your community. You may find great resources from hearing what worked for someone else in your network. "Raised on love" doesn't have an expiration date at high school commence-

Preparing for Postsecondary Success	
Postsecondary readiness (academic)	Throughout high school, the IEP team and school counselors should let you know if your child is on track to graduate. If your child is missing any credits, the school should also be able to work with you on plans for credit recovery, which may include summer school, online courses, or other credit recovery programs. There may also be special education versions of academic courses in your child's disability area. Depending on your child's postsecondary goals and the resources of your district, vocational programs may also help your child develop specific skills for their career pathway.
Postsecondary readiness (social-emotional)	Because we don't track social-emotional growth as part of a high school graduation plan, you'll want to make sure you and your school are providing your child with plenty of opportunities to grow in this area throughout high school. Extracurricular activities, part-time jobs, internships, and summer programs can help your child learn self-management, practice communication, make friends with new people, and become more independent. These are great topics to bring up at IEP meetings, particularly when working on the transition plan. Independent living skills may also factor into preparing your child for postsecondary success. Building in intentional opportunities to practice personal care, hygiene, financial management, and navigating the community are beneficial for all teenagers.
Disability services (college)	Colleges and universities do not fall under IDEA, meaning your child's IEP will not follow them to college. Instead, college and university policies on working with students with disability fall under ADA. Students must apply for accommodations through their college or university disability services office. This is almost always separate from the admissions application. Different institutions require different documentation for students to qualify for accommodations. Families are not automatically part of the process, as college students are now seen as adults. When looking at colleges, check out the disability services office, learn more about available accommodations, and make sure that you understand the process for advocating for accommodations.

Figure 21. Considerations for navigating your child's postsecondary journey.

Preparing for Postsecondary Success	
Disability services (career)	Individuals with disabilities in the workforce are protected by ADA. These protections include the ability to work free of discrimination and with "reasonable accommodations." For more information about protections in the workforce, refer to the U.S. Equal Employment Opportunity Commission.
Vocational rehabilitation	Vocational rehabilitation (VR) is a federal state program that helps individuals with disabilities find and keep employment. Students may begin working with VR in high school, and these services are also available to adults. You will want to contact your local VR department to find out more about the available resources in your area, which may include coaching, interview, and resume help, and even financial support for the training and education needed for employment.

Figure 21. Considerations for navigating your child's postsecondary journey.

ment. And at the end of the day, being raised on love doesn't mean that everything will turn out perfectly. It doesn't even guarantee that your child will be successful in school, career, or life. What it guarantees is that your child will be loved unconditionally. Although there may be a lot of heartache and drama along the way, no achievement in parenting is more important than this.

Part III

Operationalizing High Expectations

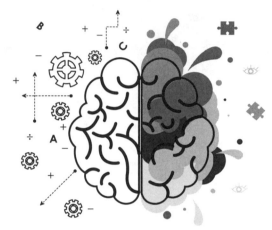

Often things that seemed impossible become possible when we nurture ambition. Look for countless ways to tell children:

> › I see you.
> › I believe in you.
> › I am cheering for you.
> › You inspire and surprise me.
> › You can do hard things.
> › Your goals, dreams, and interests matter to me.
> › We will make strengths-based decisions.
> › We are in this journey together.

Remember, we don't know what is possible until we try.

Chapter 6

High Expectations in Reading and Math

This chapter is about believing that all children can learn, grow, progress, and accomplish things that they and their communities (e.g., parents, peers, and teachers) thought were out of reach. This belief started with some thoughts I had about reading.

When I was a brand-new teacher, it never occurred to me that a child wouldn't learn how to read. Of course, I knew some children would struggle with reading. My paternal grandmother was an avid reader all of her life. When she went blind in her later years, she discovered the joy of audiobooks. My own mother is a brilliant and very slow reader whom we suspect has dyslexia. Yet, she reads novels, technical reports, the news, architectural magazines, and more.

My schema of a first-grade teacher was someone who taught children to read. When I took my first teaching job to work with first-grade students who had just completed a yearlong kindergarten program for students with profound needs, I was certain I'd teach all of them to read. Full disclosure: My understanding of reading development, cognition, and the expectations of self-contained early-childhood classrooms for students with disabilities was limited, naive, and frequently overly optimistic. Looking back, this optimism was a gift.

The expectations I had for my students were the same ones my beloved first-grade teacher, Ms. Crawford, had for me. My students and I read and wrote every day. We worked on phonics, comprehension, sight words, and storytelling. My students went home and told their families what they were reading, sang silly songs I'd made up to help them spell their names, and started pointing out sight words in books. One day, two mothers appeared in my classroom. They were astounded by what their children were learning. I looked around my cluttered, disorganized room, embarrassed by the piles of papers and scribbles on the whiteboard. Just then two students ran across the rug at top speed, colliding into an overstuffed bookshelf. You could hear the crash down the hall. I smiled at the mothers standing in my doorway and told them that I still had a lot to learn, which I did.

Six weeks or so into the school year, my students' IEPs arrived. I could not believe some of the passages I read. On more than one occasion, I checked to see if the documents were really written about the students I knew. My students had already surpassed many of the goals written in their IEPs. We were barely into October, and all of my students already could write their names and were starting to read simple sentences. They were talking (and singing) constantly, and they loved to snuggle up with books from my growing classroom library. Most were beginning to write stories and read books for early readers. These IEPs made all of that sound impossible and didn't sound like they could be about the students I worked with and cared for. Thank goodness I'd had the chance to get to know these children and jump right in with the relentless hope of a brand-new teacher before reading these IEPs. By the end of that first year, my students had self-published a bilingual book of original poetry. Except for one child who was progressing in different ways (and whose story I explore in Chapter 7), all of my students were reading, at various levels.

Children tend to meet the expectations we set for them. Often the expectations we set for children with disabilities are too low. As a new teacher, I didn't know better than to believe that my students were capable of anything they set their minds to do. I hope I never become so "educated" that I forget this lesson.

The Promise of Neuroplasticity

Teaching the children in my first class how to read shaped many of my perspectives about learning, ability, disability, and potential. In a much earlier draft of this chapter, I confidently opened with the statement, "I believe that, with love and high expectations, every child can learn how to read." I recognized that this was a bold claim, so I included a footnote about exceptions. A friend, whose son has severe cognitive disabilities, read that first draft. He gently asked me to consider at what point a child might not be able to learn how to read. "What if his IQ is 60? How about 40? I don't know the answer," he said, "but because of my son, I'm very sensitive to sweeping statements that say all students can do something."

I both heard him and desperately wanted my statement that all children could learn how to read to be true. So I set out to "prove it." First, I read articles about the neurobiology of reading, including Fumiko Hoeft's work (Konnikova, 2015). Hoeft is a cognitive neuroscientist and psychiatrist currently at the University of California. She has been studying early reading development for much of her career. Her studies have consistently found that although there are clear neural similarities between strong readers and struggling readers, these are not linked to IQ or disability/ability. In fact, much of her research has looked at a group of people she calls "stealth dyslexics" who present with all of the symptoms of dyslexia but become highly proficient readers.

Learning to read, regardless of ability/disability, is a kind of neurological miracle. Reading is a distinctly human achievement requiring an orchestrated response of several regions and functions of the brain. In an article for the Neuroscience Institute at Harvard, Edwards (2019) explained the areas of the brain involved in reading comprehension, including:

> the temporal lobe, which is responsible for phonological awareness and for decoding and discriminating sounds; Broca's area in the frontal lobe, which governs speech production and language comprehension; and the angular and supramarginal gyrus, which link different parts of the brain so that letter shapes can be put together to form words. In addition, there are several important white-matter pathways involved in reading. (para. 4–5)

When you snuggle up with your child and read a book, you are able to engage these different regions of the brain without giving much (or any) thought to the neurology behind it. You work on recognizing letters and letter sounds. You build vocabulary. You teach patterns. You model reading. And as you do this, the neural pathways in your child's brain become stronger and able to master independent reading. Research on struggling readers has shown that through practice, intervention, and supports, educators can help students strengthen the brain regions needed for reading (Meyler, Keller, Cherkassky, Gabrieli, & Just, 2008). Eric Kandel was awarded a Nobel Prize in Medicine in 2000 for his pioneering work around how learning rewires the brain (Doidge, 2016). This is the promise of neuroplasticity. Neuroplasticity is the ability to strengthen the neural connections in the brain through learning practice. This is how we are able to gain and retain new skills. Carol Dweck (2006), a Stanford psychologist, used this concept in her work on growth mindset.

Next, I reached out to neurologists, medical professionals, teachers, and nurses. Sometimes I opened with my story about teaching that first classroom of children to read; other times I dove right in to the question: "In your professional opinion, what conditions (if any) make it so that a person cannot learn functional reading skills?" The professionals who responded offered knowledge, warmth, and well-placed curiosity about this question. Their answers tended toward personal experience more than scientific study. They usually told me about a cousin, a niece, or a neighbor. They shared personal stories of people they love who have complex disabilities and who did not grow up to be readers. We talked about other progress these people had made, the strengths they had, and most importantly, all of the reasons and ways they were loved. We talked about picture boards, assistive technology, and text messages sent using emoji instead of words. We talked a lot about love. Yet, I wondered, could these young people have learned to read had they had other supports in the classroom?

When I am puzzling through something, I often go to a group dance class at our local gym. One evening I took these thoughts with me for 45 minutes of choreographed cardio. Looking around the studio, I noticed that a retired teacher who had worked with students with medical needs, a local varsity cheerleader who has Down syndrome, and the cheerleader's mother were all in class. Eureka! This felt like a gift. What if I pulled these three people together after class for a focus group on reading development? Yes, I resolved, leaping across the studio.

And then, by some wise strike of grace, I reconsidered.

What would we gain from this conversation? What exactly was I trying to prove, and why was I so set on proving it? One of the songs we danced to had some particularly tricky choreography. After class, I saw the cheerleader laughing with her mother. She was showing her how to keep her arms bent while also twirling her hands upward. They were both having a great time. That is when it occurred to me that this student's reading level had little to do with the things that matter most, such as happiness, belonging, and love.

I gave the two of them a high five and drove home.

My mind replayed a conversation I'd had earlier that day with Stephanie, a school administrator. When I had asked her my "reading question," she told me about her close relationship with her nephew, a young man with autism. And then she said, "Kathryn, what question is your book really trying to answer? Is the question about reading level or math level, or is it about a more contextualized understanding of high expectations?"

I went to sleep that night thinking about this.

Setting High Expectations

The next morning, I took the last drink of my coffee, which had gone cold, and rushed out the door for church. In the pews was a family whom I didn't know well. Their son, who is grown, uses a power chair and has limited use of his body. The pastor placed a communion wafer in his mouth for him. Suddenly I saw how me writing a footnote about exceptions missed the most important point. Worse, it was inconsistent with the inclusive values I'd tried to build this book around. This book celebrates children who learn differently. These chapters reject the boxes we put students in and recognize that children learn at different paces and in different ways. Although grounded in love and high expectations, my statement about *all children reading* could be one of those boxes we want to avoid.

Are there conditions that make it so a person cannot learn functional reading skills? Of course there are. Proving (or disproving) this does not serve children or families. Instead, the more important gift is to see our children's unique strengths and to support them with high expectations and love as they find their way.

This belief in the power of high expectations is deeply rooted in my core philosophy around parenting and teaching, particularly for children who learn differently. I have also been wounded personally and professionally by those whose expectations for children with disabilities are far too low. I believe that children often meet the expectations we set for them, and that we don't know what is possible until we try. High expectations mean that, with hard work, support, and love, our children can accomplish tasks that seem unlikely or even impossible. We must communicate this belief to our children and then help them get there, even when getting there takes a long time. Sometimes this looks like learning to read. Sometimes it looks like learning how to make a friend. Sometimes it looks like independent living skills and/or reaching other meaningful goals. Remember, caring for children with disabilities is often about the long game.

What seems unlikely or even impossible is contextualized. A few weeks after that Sunday, I noticed a photo of the young man I had wanted to get to know in our church bulletin. Following the photo was an article about a large-scale recycling initiative he was leading (with his parents' help). At our next church service, I was proud to congratulate him on these efforts and to spend some time visiting with his family.

Although the focus of this chapter is on the academic skills of reading and math, the heart of high expectations extends to social-emotional and independent living skills. Further, these skills are not a consolation prize. Many different skills matter. In fact, I know many children who are highly proficient readers and who struggle to make a friend, turn in homework, or remember to brush their teeth every day. High expectations are about believing that children are capable of more and supporting young people to accomplish the things that are challenging for them. It's about not giving up.

Throughout this chapter, I'll share stories of exceptional children I have worked with, including several who have now graduated high school as readers and whose parents were told that they would likely never learn how to read or how to read well. Before we dive in, I want to offer one more reminder about pacing. We know that for our children who learn differently, their paths are often colored by learning at a different pace from their peers. *When* a child learns a skill is far less important than our unwavering belief that a child *will* learn.

Learning to Read: Research-Based Strategies

One of my closest friends has a daughter who is learning to read. Lately, every time we get together, he asks me exasperated questions about sight words and phonics: "Her first-grade teacher is making her memorize how to spell the numbers from 1–10. Have you ever thought about how we spell *eight*? What the hell?"

He's right. There is a lot of information to sort through, and yes, the English language is full of exceptions to rules. Learning to read requires multilayered skills that promote positive development, cognitive growth, and creative thinking. A different way to think about this is that learning to read has social and academic benefits beyond just learning to read. I developed *Page Mapping* (see Figure 22) to help parents (and teachers) prioritize research-based strategies consistently shown to support children who are learning to read. These are the strategies I've used in my home and classrooms. To build on our conversation from earlier, these activities are important and beneficial for all children, regardless of ability/disability.

In fact, reading together promotes positive health and development. Pediatrician Robert Needlman worked on ways to center literacy in his primary care practice (McNabb, 2016). Why? Because he believed that "listening to stories changes the structure of the human brain, contributes to the brain's health, strengthens a child's attachment to his or her parents, and increases overall emotional health and resilience" (para. 4). Particularly for children (of any age) who are not *yet* reading, listening to stories and read alouds promotes positive brain development.

The bedtime story has sustained the test of time because it works in helping grow both relationships and readers. How you model these strategies for your children can also have an impact on their development as readers and learners. Children are always watching. I was working on my Ph.D. coursework when our daughter was only 2 years old. This meant that Saturdays and Sundays included countless hours studying. It wasn't long before our toddler started "highlighting" her board books, too. It's essential for young people to see *you* reading and to hear you talk about what you're learning from books, newspapers, and magazines.

Although books and access to text are important, reading grows through a variety of skills that happen outside of simply working through a book. Music, patterns, and art have all been shown to help young children develop the capacities they need as new readers. Sing, paint, notice patterns, and practice routines together. Think, create, and laugh together. These strategies are important for your child's development, and they can also be gifts for your relationship. However, Page Mapping isn't an algorithm for a quick path to success. It takes years to develop as a reader. Stay the course. Remember, parenting tends to focus on the long game.

At Their Own Pace

It seems that as soon as you become a parent, you are presented with lists of developmental milestones and target timelines. There is a lot of pressure for your child to be "on track," or better yet, "ahead of schedule." When your child learns or develops differently, this pressure can feel particularly intense. As an educator, I often remind concerned parents that

Page Mapping	
Immerse yourself in PAGES *Strategies to help families support prereading*	
P	Play with words and sounds through singing and rhyming.
A	Ask questions to encourage story sharing (both real and make-believe).
G	Give your child a variety of texts to explore.
E	Engage in dialogue about what you are reading.
S	Sit together and read every day.
Here is a MAP to help you on your way *Mindsets to foster reading and problem solving*	
M	Mistakes and learning new skills are things to celebrate.
A	Art activates imagination.
P	Patterns and routines prime the brain for logic.

Figure 22. Research-based strategies and mindsets to support reading.

even with our best efforts, children will learn at their own pace. A few years ago, I got to eat my words, again. My daughter was well into first grade and wasn't reading at all. I took her for her well-child checkup, and her pediatrician (whom I adore) was flabbergasted and concerned. Here was a child with the vocabulary of a fifth grader who couldn't read a simple sentence. I mumbled something about asynchronous development. The pediatrician asked if we had a family history of dyslexia, which we do.

"Do you read to her at home?" he asked gently.

Did we read to her at home? Lilah had grown up on the Page Mapping strategies since day one! Actually, since *before* day one. I may be a bit of a perfectionist. While we are dispelling myths, let me dispel another: Perfectionism has little to do with parental success.

All through kindergarten and far into first grade, Lilah wasn't interested in learning to read. She was interested in science, math, animals, and art. She orchestrated complex and strange-smelling "chemistry experiments" on our back deck. She asked for math workbooks for presents. Although she would snuggle up for me to read a book to her, and although she liked to look through the pictures in books, she had no interest in reading words on her own. None.

I scheduled a conference with her teacher who said, "Yes, Lilah is behind her peers in reading, but I'm not worried." Her teacher smiled at me. "Children learn at a variety of paces," she said, reassuringly patting my arm.

I took a deep breath. *Yes, I know.*

Then, this wholehearted teacher (Fishman-Weaver, 2018b) continued to read with Lilah in class. She was patient and unwavering in her belief that our daughter would learn to read. And one day, Lilah became interested in reading. Late in the spring, she came home and read us an early reader. By the next month, she was into simple chapter books. The summer after first grade, she read . . . everything. We joke that she now has the most used library card in our city.

A wholehearted teacher, a newfound interest, and the momentum of success helped our daughter learn quickly. Yes, she started reading a bit later than her peers, but once she started reading, she took off. I've worked with students who made uneven progress, experienced a huge breakthrough, and then hit a plateau that lasted for months. I've also worked with children who have made consistent, slow, steady progress.

Sometimes these students stay on the early reading books for a long time. Then, they try a slightly harder book, find it too hard, try again, eventually work through that book, then go on to the next, and so on. Sometimes their progress is so steady we miss that is even happening until one day we step back and notice they are reading a passage that would have been impossible a year before. "When did this happen?" we ask.

There isn't a right path or pace. With appropriate supports, children tend to learn at just the right pace for them. There are some important things we can do to help set the stage, build skill sets, normalize mistake making, and foster a love of learning. Many of these specifics are suggested in the Page Mapping shared previously. Although these practices matter, at the end of the day nothing matters more than an unwavering commitment that, through love and high expectations, our children will indeed get there.

Reading Passport

Have you ever visited another country or place very different from where you live? Sometimes all goes smoothly; all you need are your airline tickets and your passport. Yes, you might experience some jet lag, but if you just follow the crowds, without too much trouble you will find that you have arrived at your destination. Other times, though, the flight is delayed, the trailhead is not clearly marked, or your rental car breaks down on the freeway in the middle of the night. When someone finally gives you a map, it is in a language you can't make sense of. With faith, effort, and maybe a few choice words or behaviors along the way, eventually, you also arrive.

What happens after you arrive? You clean up and step outside into a new environment. Suddenly you have a whole new sensory world to learn and explore. It takes lots of energy and street smarts to navigate the new infrastructure, culture, foods, customs, and language. Although some strategies translate from place to place, you find that each location has its own nuance and charm. An encouraging tour guide or local friend can be a lifesaver in navigating this new city.

All of this is, of course, a metaphor for learning how to read. Reading is a complex skill that develops over time. It is often as much about the journey as it is the destination. Do you remember learning how to read? For some of us, our path was so straightforward it's hard to remember. For others, the answer is more complicated and holistic. There was struggle, uncertainty, and small moments of breakthrough that eventually led to making sense of a short board book, and then another early reader, and so on.

Learning to read is part of a lifelong journey. How confident would you feel if I asked you to analyze a Shakespearean sonnet? How about a medical journal? What about a text in a language you haven't studied since high school? I suspect that at least one of these readings would cause you some anxiety. Tackling an unfamiliar genre can be a great lesson in empathy as your own child learns to read. When I worked with reading tutors for developing or struggling readers, I often asked them to read Lewis Carroll's (1871) "The Jabberwocky" for exactly this purpose. The famous nonsensical poem begins:

> 'Twas brillig, and the slithy toves
> Did gyre and gimble in the wabe:
> All mimsy were the borogoves,
> And the mome raths outgrabe.

This poem offers a nice springboard for conversations about the difference between decoding and comprehension. Sometimes we don't realize we're lost until someone asks us to pause and say where we are.

Remember the previous example with the unmarked trailhead or the rental car that overheated on the freeway? Even after you arrive at your destination, your adventures in reading seldom follow perfectly prescribed paths. You veer left when you see a sign pointing to the ocean. You stop at a fruit stand on the road and bargain for a bag of mangos. You might see things that others miss; if you don't, your children will. Join your children for their reading journeys. Ask them questions about books: What do they notice? What do they think will happen next? What do they think a character is feeling? I bet you will be surprised by what you discover on this journey together.

The Importance of Choice in Reading

I spent 2 years running the literacy intervention class at a local public high school. Students were assigned to this class because they had been identified as *struggling readers*. On standardized reading tests, the students in my program were all behind their peers. However, the common issue I identified with this group was not lack of aptitude for reading skills. Instead, it was lack of motivation to engage with the books that had been offered to them in school. My students were what we sometimes call reluctant readers of literature. What is the best way to engage someone who is disinterested in reading? Engage the person—end of sentence.

The way we can do that is by connecting young people to high-interest, relevant texts. Who's the best person to pick these out? You guessed it—the person who will be reading the text. Maybe children are into sports, video games, cars, rocket ships, or cooking (the list goes on). The great news is that, whatever the interest, there are books on that subject. In an article on engaging reluctant readers, Scales (2005) wrote, "The answer is simple: Know the students, know the books, and seek creative ways to connect the two" (para. 4). This is where we step in as parents. Young people don't always know how to find books or texts that match their preferences. We might not have a working knowledge of every book about the Jurassic era either, but we can find a great media specialist or teacher who can help. We can search online for books on the topics our children are interested in. We can find the answers to their questions. We can also make different kinds of texts available to our children.

When I made a newspaper available in my literacy intervention class, I was often surprised by how many of the students chose to read it. Many of them were athletes who especially loved the sports section. Others enjoyed the comics, job postings, and the education section when there was an article about a school, teacher, or student they knew. This brings us to the relevance factor. Readers want to see themselves in the pages of the books they read. In Chapter 7, we will talk about the importance of representation. As you are looking for reading material for your child, consider the identities and experiences of the characters in the books you choose. Are there similarities between your child and the racial, ethnic, age, ability/disability, culture, and gender identities of the characters? Can your children identify with and see themselves in the pages of their books? The protagonists and heroes you expose children to in literature influence both their engagement and self-perception. Who shows up on your child's bookshelf matters.

Spend more time thinking about content and connection than you do reading level. This isn't to say that reading level doesn't matter; it does. However, it's not as good a predictor of engagement as choice and subject matter. Children can benefit from reading a book at a lower level that captures their interests. Children are also often willing to stretch themselves through a high-interest text that is just outside of their reading level. Further, parents may also be mistaken in our assessments of children's true reading ability. Maybe we just haven't found the right book yet.

Hank was a football player in my literacy intervention class. He weighed close to 400 pounds and was the happiest guy I knew. One day, his English teacher came to speak to me in an angry panic. She wanted to know why he was in her general education class "because he clearly doesn't know how to read." I looked at her confused. Just 2 hours before, Hank and I had been reading an article on football strategy. She didn't believe me. The next day, I got the three of us together and asked if Hank would read a little of the football article to us.

"Sure," he said, and read without struggle.

Hank could read. However, he didn't connect with the texts in his junior year literature class. He also didn't yet have a lot of scholarly confidence and was therefore reluctant to participate in his literature class. His teachers and family could help his academic self-esteem grow or flounder. Had he and I not found the texts on football strategy, or had his English teacher not heard him read that afternoon, it is possible that more teachers would have thought Hank "wasn't a reader" or worse that he wasn't capable of reading. Let's encourage each other to be very careful about the assumptions we make and the things we say about our children who learn differently.

Psychologist Lev Vygotsky (1978) developed a concept called *zone of proximal development* (ZPD), which refers to that magical place between what a learner can do without support and what a learner can almost do without support. Identifying books and challenges in a student's ZPD matters. These are the texts and tasks that stretch children (and adults) to learn and grow. Experiencing success in the ZPD, often requires the support, encouragement, and guidance of what Vygotsky called "a more knowledgeable other." With reading support, this may be the parent who tells a child what an unfamiliar word means, the teacher who takes turns reading with their students, or even a sibling who discusses a section with their sister. We also should not discount children's assessments of their own ZPD when it comes to reading. When we give our children ownership over their reading (and learning), the results are often surprisingly positive.

One of my greatest parental achievements may have been developing a love of pleasure reading in both of our children. Pleasure reading, or reading for pure enjoyment, leads to numerous developmental benefits. Howard (2011) found that "pleasure reading fulfills three broad functions: it enhanced academic performance, social engagement and personal development" (p. 46). My husband and I built reading for enjoyment into our everyday home schedule by giving our children choice in reading and ample time for bedtime reading. When our children were very young, they chose the books we read aloud to them. Then, after we'd said our goodnights, we gave them extra time to look through these books, plus two or three more that they chose on their own. Our children were 100% in charge of choosing the books. That meant if they wanted to reread *Corduroy Goes to the Doctor* for the 573rd time in a month, we read again about how "the waiting room has toys and books" (Freeman, 2005, p. 2). If they wanted to read a magazine article on the life cycle of ladybugs, we went with it. On the weekends, we relaxed our time parameters and let our children stay up as late as they wanted reading. As long as they were in their beds and looking at or reading books, that time was theirs. As they became more proficient readers, they traded their picture books for chapter books, and then for novels. Their beds were lined with pillows and blankets and graphic novels, biographies of rappers, and stories of dragon slayers. I wouldn't have chosen many of these books to read myself, and that is okay. As Anderson (2016) wrote about the importance of choice in reading, "Intrinsic motivation flows from ownership" (p. 16). Children are often attached to the books they choose for themselves, and this attachment translates to more reading engagement, which translates to increased reading development.

Self-Fulfilling Prophecy: Math as an Example

In psychology, *self-fulfilling prophecy* is the connection between beliefs, expectations, and outcomes. That is, if we think something will come true, it often does. If we think we will fail a math test, we just might do that. If we think we'll knock our speech out of the park, it's more likely to go well. This idea has been extended to incorporate the effect that key adults' (e.g., parents' and teachers') perceptions of children can also have on performance. Ackerman's (2018) findings suggest that teacher expectations of students had more influence on student performance than did differences in talent or intelligence. What does this have to do with math in general and math expectations for students with disabilities in particular? Quite a lot.

Math, perhaps more than any other subject, seems shrouded in beliefs about who can (and, by proxy, who can't) do math. Just as in our conversation about reading, disability may contribute to complications and nuances around math achievement. For example, *dyscalculia* is a condition similar to dyslexia that directly interferes with the brain's ability to make sense of numbers and number concepts. However, just as in our conversation with reading, we don't know what's possible until we try it. Over and over again I've found that students, including students with or without disabilities, are more able to solve complex math problems than their teachers (or even parents) thought possible. How we talk about math, normalize math thinking in our daily lives, and encourage our students to engage with numbers, patterns, and shapes can go a long way to foster mathematical thinking and alleviate some of the widespread math anxiety we see in children (and adults).

While I was teaching in a self-contained elementary classroom for students with moderate disabilities, the district launched a new, rigorous, standards-based math curriculum. I went straight to my principal and asked to be included. My class became the first self-contained special education classroom in the district to adopt the new curriculum. I got my students excited about the new math learning we were going to do. I said we were going to learn multiplication and division, and keep math journals. I told them the truth—that I couldn't wait to get started. And guess what? Neither could they.

We worked through every lesson in the third-grade curriculum. Yes, I made a few accommodations along the way, as I would have done for any class of learners. Sometimes we held an extra review session. Sometimes I made up a silly song to go along with the lesson, and sometimes my students had support in writing their answers after they told them to a paraprofessional. Along the way, I was intentionally over-the-top excited for math. We talked about my favorite math facts (which, not coincidentally, were the ones my students had the hardest time remembering). Soon you could hear the students saying, "Oh, 7 squared! Mrs. K loves that one. It's 49."

Administrators, teachers, and specialists came to see the mathematicians in my class. Several were astounded by both the enthusiasm and aptitude my students had for math. Practice, support, and framing can reshape how we think about learning and, more importantly, how our children think about themselves as learners. What happens when we expect that our children can read that chapter book, solve that division problem, or join that new class? As with my class of excited math learners, often students can do the very thing some thought they couldn't. A few years later, I got to test out this theory with older students as well.

Algebra Scholars: High Expectations in High School Math

"Kathryn, we need a new teacher for several sections of mathematics and finance for high school students with IEPs."

I considered this for a few minutes. I'd always liked math . . .

"Okay. I'm in!"

"Great!" my principal said, casually adding that there wasn't an established curriculum or set of standards for my mathematics course. "It will be okay," she assured me. "You have the summer to figure it out."

Because this was a high school, algebra skills seemed like a good place to start.

I spent June, July, and August reviewing every algebra and prealgebra book I could find. I made it my goal to develop a class that would give students the math skills they needed to go from my class into the general education algebra series. Therefore, I worked backward from our district's algebra course to develop a scope and sequence that taught positive and negative integers, basics of equations, adding and subtracting fractions, and working with exponents. I introduced beginning algebra concepts, including order of operations, graphing inequalities, evaluating functions, and working with slope intercept.

A few people heard about my "rigorous" plans and balked. Someone even told me rather aggressively that this was never supposed to be a "real math class." Feeling both angry and confused, I went home and cooked my family a giant dinner (a personal self-care strategy for me). I thought about this person's comments and decided that my students would prove all of the doubters wrong. Love and high expectations are about believing in children enough to give them interesting and creative work, as well as the encouragement that they can do such work. High school math didn't seem like the place to start making exceptions to my core educational philosophy. Was I relentless and tenacious? Absolutely. When it comes to your kids, I bet you are, too.

I returned to school in August for professional development and shared my lesson plans with a few colleagues. A few people exchanged glances that were becoming familiar. I was far enough into my teaching career to both read those looks and know better than to lower my expectations. I walked into that first class excited to tell my students they were taking a combined prealgebra/algebra course. This framing was a profound shift from the special education (or remedial or intervention) math course they thought they "had been put in." When I announced my plans, the students sat up taller in their seats, raised their chins, and looked at me like I was 100% nuts.

"Oh, it won't be easy," I said, agreeing. "But I'll help you every step of the way, and I know you all can do it."

The district math coordinator had helped me find some old algebra textbooks. I distributed them to the class. Our first lesson was on variables.

One of my students raised his hand. "Is this for real? There aren't animals or other baby stuff on these math sheets."

"Yes, dear, you're in a real math class now."

And they were. We worked hard (so hard) all year. We puzzled over interesting problems. We studied diverse mathematicians, including mathematicians of color and mathematicians with disabilities. We did extra practice problems before school. We took a second look at problems we didn't understand. We demonstrated equations on the board. We talked about growth mindset (Dweck, 2006). We celebrated Pi Day. We talked about math and thought of ourselves as mathematicians all year long. My paraprofessionals said that they had never seen the excitement and success these students experienced.

We were a diverse group of student mathematicians. Many of my students had never taken a general education math class. We had students who needed one-on-one paraprofessional support, students who had severe medical needs in addition to learning disabilities, students of diverse ages, students who lived in foster care, students who were constantly in trouble, and students who fit two or more of these categories. However, in our class, none of these identities were as salient as our collective identity as "algebra scholars."

At the end of the year, most of the ninth- and 10th-grade students were reintegrated into the algebra track with their general education peers, something that hadn't happened before this class. My 11th- and 12th-grade students graduated or took career classes, and they all went on to use these math skills in life. Once again, administrators and coordinators at the district level noticed the "uncommon success" in my math class, and they asked me to join a work group on developing higher standards for high school math classes that served students with disabilities.

Impossibly Possible

One evening, my husband and I had some friends over for dinner. I told them about my math class. One of our guests shared that Krista, her sister, had profound disabilities. Her sister had never taken a class like mine, but if she had, this guest wasn't sure she would have been successful. I told her that many of my students' families were similarly shocked by the caliber of math my students were doing (and, on our best days, even enjoying).

Our dinner guest was quiet for a long time, and then she said, "What if Krista could have done this all along, and we just didn't know it was possible?"

That question has stayed with me. Of course, it's one I can't answer. Even if I could, Krista is grown now. If I met with her family today, I would tell them to focus on what's still to come, not what might have been. Still, this question about possibility is the same one I chased at the beginning of the chapter. We don't know what is possible until we try. My experiences in education (and parenting) have taught me that more is almost always possible. I encourage you to keep the ideas of the naysayers at a safe distance, even when those ideas come from individuals you love and respect. In my experience, children prove adults wrong every day.

Let's keep nurturing our children's ambition and reminding them that they are absolutely capable of doing hard things, learning new concepts, and growing as both learners and human beings. My hope is that you can be the voice of love and high expectations in your child's head. Although I can't tell you what specific skills your children will master, I know that with these beliefs, your children will inspire, impress, and surprise you again and again.

Chapter 7

Exceptional Children, Different Learners

Luiza is articulate, kind, and one of the warmest people you will ever meet. Whenever I asked general education teachers if Luiza could join them for an afternoon, they were enthusiastic about including her. As she is cooperative and positive, it was easy to mainstream her for classes with her general education peers. She listened attentively and was quick to make friends. Everyone was drawn to her. Although she was a joy to have in class, Luiza couldn't complete any of our assignments without a lot of scaffolded one-on-one help coupled with significant modifications. She had severe cognitive disabilities. I had the privilege of being her teacher from the time she was 7 until she was 10 years old. Although this was a decade ago, I still think of her often and wonder about the outcome of a placement decision we made at the end of third grade.

In the years she was in my class, her IEP team worked hard to help Luiza develop her functional reading and math skills. She made progress, and the team celebrated. However, at the end of third grade, her academic skills were still a long way from those of her age-group peers, including those in our classroom. After she had been in my classroom program from first to third grade, I was asked to recommend the most appropriate type of fourth-grade classroom. There were three options:

> › Luiza could continue in a self-contained classroom for students with mild to moderate disabilities in a different school,
> › she could move to a classroom for students with moderate to profound disabilities in a different school, or

> she could enroll in a general education fourth-grade classroom with some specialist support and stay at her current school.

Our district didn't have the resources for a full-time paraprofessional, and Luiza's family couldn't send her to a private school.

Luiza's family had recently immigrated to the United States. Navigating our public education system was challenging, even without the added complications of special education services. Luiza's mother said that she trusted my recommendation. I felt the weight of this decision and struggled to make the best possible choice. In thinking about free and appropriate public education (FAPE), I felt that Luiza could benefit from any of the three options. However, in considering the least restrictive environment (LRE), the self-contained options didn't feel like the right fit. As an IEP team, we had a choice that we often face in working with children who learn differently. We can make our decisions based on limitations or based on strengths. Given the choice of the two, strengths-based decisions tend to better serve kids.

This isn't always an "either/or" approach. Sometimes we have to focus on the disability area and remediate what isn't going well. In these instances, measurable goals can be extremely useful. Figure 23 gives a holistic look at the guiding questions we can ask as we put these strengths-based support plans in place. With Luiza, the team chose to focus on her interpersonal strengths. The team recommended that she start fourth grade in a general education class at the school where she was already deeply loved with some specialist support. Before the next school year started, my family and I moved to a new district in a new state. This was in the age before social media, and Luiza's mother's phone number changed frequently. So, although I've thought about her often, I don't know how Luiza's fourth-grade year unfolded. Did we make the right decision? Was there a "right decision" to make in this case? I don't think it is that simple.

When faced with complicated decisions, choose inclusion and strength. As we explored in Chapter 6, we often don't know what our children are capable of until we give them the opportunity to try. In this chapter, we'll explore how exceptionality and difference inform the decisions we make about our children and how love and high expectations can be a compass along the way.

When we base our decisions on children's strengths, we . . .	When we base our decisions on children's limitations, we . . .
› Focus on what they can do. › Pay attention to their gifts and talents. › Leverage things that are working well. › Listen to their ideas and preferences. › Listen to a team, including the children themselves, about how to support, normalize, and include children in the least restrictive environment possible. › Consider opportunities where they will excel. › Spend a lot of time exploring what lights them up and helps them succeed. › Set goals that are focused on their interests and passions, even if those are hard to measure.	› Focus on what they struggle with. › Pay attention to their limitations. › Leverage our energies to respond to what isn't working well. › Listen to professionals who can support, accommodate, or remediate disabilities or deficits. › Consider environments where they will have peers who have similar challenges. › Spend a lot of time exploring what isn't going the way we want and how we wish these children were performing. › Set measurable goals that are focused on the disability area.

Figure 23. Strengths-based decisions.

Exceptional Children

In education and psychology, *exceptional children* is an umbrella term for young people who develop, think, behave, and/or learn in significantly different ways than their age-level peers. This includes children who receive gifted education services, children who receive special education services, and twice-exceptional children who receive both of these types of services. Having taught and worked with children in all of these areas, I now have a better understanding for why so many types of exceptionality are often referenced together: Being different makes us similar.

In schools where students are grouped by age and asked to meet grade-level expectations according to birthdate, learning differently is a shared, special trait. Sometimes this special trait feels more like a burden than a gift. Most of our systems and processes in schools were set up for sameness, instead of difference or exceptionality. Our children who learn at a different pace, who see things with a new perspective, or who navigate development nonlinearly, often feel like they are driving in the opposite direction on a one-way street. For families and children, this can be nerve-racking, frustrating, and scary. If we pause, though, and zoom out from the one-way street crisis, we'll find that caring for and learning from children who learn differently can be an exceptional opportunity for us all.

Neurodiversity

What if we didn't approach disability as something to fix or cure? What if we didn't frame disability around what a person can't do or struggles to do? What if, instead, we approached disability as something to affirm and celebrate? What if we thought about disability in terms of the unique skills and perspectives this identity presents? These are some of the essential questions neurodiversity scholars consider.

Neurodiversity is a relatively new way of looking at disability, and it is gaining traction from scientists and advocates alike. *Neurodiversity* refers to the belief that differences and disabilities are part of normal—and even beneficial—variance among people. Whereas traditional perspectives on disability may have been categorized as deficit models, neurodiversity offers a strengths-based approach. This means that instead of focusing on what is wrong, broken, or lacking in people with disabilities, neurodiversity advocates and researchers focus on what is special, enhanced, or added by the presence of a disability. For example, research on autism has shown that many people on the autism spectrum have a heightened ability to recognize patterns, enhanced memory, and strength in mathematics (Armstrong, 2015; Crespi, 2016; Iuculano et al., 2014). Research on ADHD points to the high energy, creativity, enthusiasm, and hyperfocus that individuals with ADHD sometimes exhibit. In fact, Hartnett, Nelson, and Rinn (2004) even suggested that gifted individuals are sometimes misdiagnosed with ADHD due to the similarities between how gifted students and students with ADHD process information in complex and creative ways. This is similar to Honos-Webb's (2010) work on "the gift of ADHD." Many celebrities, particularly in the performing arts, have ADHD (Nall, 2016).

Rethinking the Master Schedule

Ryan was a young man at a high school where I used to teach. At this high school, we used a block schedule of four 90-minute classes daily. One year we added a new homeroom program to our schedule for 30 minutes daily. Homeroom followed one of two lunch shifts. We had more than 2,000 students at our school. Figuring out the logistics of this master schedule required advanced operational skills, but our administrative team managed to put an initial schedule together that worked.

And then we had our first assembly day. How were we going to reorganize our schedule to accommodate the assembly, keep homeroom, and not have students eating lunch at 9:00 a.m. or 2:00 p.m.?

Enter Ryan.

At the time, Ryan was a sophomore. At 16, he already knew more about our high school than probably anyone else in the building, including the veteran teachers and the principal. For example, Ryan knew all of faculty and staff by full legal names (and maiden names), the schedules we taught (including which hour and for which class), our hobbies, and most certainly, any time a teacher had broken a rule (such as making too many copies, parking in a visitor spot, or allowing students to study in a teacher work space). A fervent rule-follower, Ryan wasn't shy about calling us out on any of these infractions. He also wasn't shy about telling us about his big ideas for organizing the school. And his ideas were really, really good. Two days before the first assembly, Ryan e-mailed all of the faculty and staff. (How he got the e-mail list, I have no idea.) Attached to the e-mail was a schedule he had worked out for organizing the four classes, two lunch shifts, homerooms, and the assembly. He'd also proactively created schedules for other special days that we hadn't planned for yet, such as testing days and early release days. The schedules were brilliant.

For the next 3 years, Ryan was our de facto scheduler and became an assistant to our administrator in charge of operations. Ryan would regularly e-mail the entire faculty and staff with special schedules and posters reminding us of any rules that he noticed people were struggling to follow. If, for example, there was a teacher workroom adjacent to my classroom, and if I consistently allowed students work there, Ryan would leave posters on my desk that spelled out in block letters, "This is a teacher workspace only." If I didn't hang the posters myself, I could be sure that Ryan would gladly tape them up for me the next morning.

Ryan has an advanced ability to organize complex schedules; likewise, several major companies are starting to consider ways that neurodiverse teams can make their businesses and organizations more effective. According to the *Harvard Business Review* (Austin & Pisano, 2017), companies that are actively pursuing neurodiversity as a competitive advantage include SAP, Hewlett Packard Enterprise (HPE), Microsoft, Willis Towers Watson, Ford, and EY. Others, such as Caterpillar, Dell Technologies, Deloitte, IBM, JPMorgan Chase, and UBS, are beginning to follow suit. I believe that neurodiversity also gives schools a competitive advantage, including unmatched opportunities for practicing empathy, communication, inclusion, and creative problem solving.

To summarize, neurodiversity is a research movement aimed at:

> › normalizing disability within a broader discussion of diversity, and
> › flipping the script on how we view and talk about ability/disability.

Instead of trying to fix or cure people, those in the neurodiversity movement want to support, accommodate, and affirm. As Nicolaidis (2012) explained, "The neurodiversity movement challenges us to rethink [disability] through the lens of human diversity. It asks us to value diversity in neurobiological development as we would value diversity in gender, race, ethnicity, religion, or sexual orientation" (para. 3). Your child's school may or may not have a background in neurodiversity. If the school is not familiar with this concept, my hope is the information in this chapter will help families work with professionals on reframing the conversation about our children who learn differently. Families can highlight the skills their children bring to the classroom (e.g., programming, kindness, memory, etc.), the strengths they possess (e.g., pattern recognition, athletics, empathy, etc.), and the ways that schools are richer for including and affirming neurodiverse students.

Representation: Neurodiverse Role Models

Learning more about the works and contributions of neurodiverse people is important for everyone. It reframes the ways we think about ability and disability. For children who learn differently, neurodiverse representation is particularly empowering. It's also missing from many classrooms. As a family advocate, you can both change that conversation at home and offer stories and suggestions for your child's classroom teacher to include more neurodiverse representation at school. The following are four examples of amazing individuals whose biographies I've introduced in my house and classrooms. I choose these four for their gender, disability, and professional diversity. Three are contemporary, and one is an individual known for his different thinking in the 1400s. These four represent a *tiny* fraction of the neurodiverse role models that you can learn about with your child:

› **Dr. Temple Grandin** (b. 1947) is a leading authority on autism and animal livestock behavior. She openly credits her autism for enabling her to excel in both of these areas of expertise. Grandin writes, publishes, and lectures widely on how her ability to learn differently allows her to "think in pictures" (Grandin, 2006), understand animals, and notice things that others miss. Grandin holds a professor position at Colorado State University. She has written several books, including books for families on supporting children with autism. I have shared the HBO original movie *Temple Grandin* with high school students to help them learn more about Grandin's life and work and to open up conversations about autism and learning differently.

› **Leonardo da Vinci** (1452–1519) was a famous painter, inventor, and sculptor. His famous works include *The Mona Lisa* and *The Last Supper*, as well as designs for a tank, mechanical robot, helicopter, and parachute. Many of da Vinci's ideas were hundreds of years ahead of their time. He is well-known for his ability to think differently as well as his affection for writing backward. Some researchers have speculated that he had dyslexia and ADHD, and that these disabilities directly contributed to his ability to see things in new ways.

› **John Lee Cronin** (b. 1996) is an entrepreneur. He is the cofounder and inspiration for John's Crazy Socks[19], a sock company he runs with his dad. In addition to creative socks, the company offers personalized customer service, including handwritten notes to customers and thank-you cards to active military. Cronin has Down syndrome, and his company primarily employs people with disabilities: "Part of our goal at John's Crazy Socks is to empower people and demonstrate the possibilities that each of us

---

19 If visiting the website (https://johnscrazysocks.com) with young children, I recommend selecting the examples in advance, as a few have adult humor or language.

possesses" (John's Crazy Socks, 2019, para. 1). The company has been recognized nationally and internationally, and a portion of all proceeds goes the Special Olympics.

› **Terezinha Guilhermina** (b. 1978) is a Brazilian athlete and world record-holding Paralympic sprinter. Guilhermina is blind. She usually races blindfolded and with a guide. Given her incredible speed, finding a fast enough guide has been a challenge. In the 2016 Olympics in Rio, she ran some events with Usain Bolt[20]. Guilhermina grew up living in poverty. In fact, she only tried running for the first time when her sister lent her a pair of sneakers, as the family couldn't afford two pairs (Gittings, 2013). Guilhermina is an outstanding role model of the power of potential, persistence, and drive. Celebrating Paralympic athletes, including Guilhermina, can offer children (and adults) inspiring lessons in strength.

Expose your children to neurodiverse role models who are achieving at high levels in their areas, advocating for inclusion and disability rights, and celebrating their unique abilities and perspectives. Seek out children's books with neurodiverse characters and read biographies of neurodiverse individuals. Help young people see that there is a rich community and culture of people who learn differently, and that this community has been responsible for significant contributions in all sectors of society. In some cases, these achievements may not have been possible were it not for the ability to think, learn, and see things in different ways. The more we can celebrate neurodiverse role models and reframe disability using a strengths-based approach, the more our children who learn differently will feel supported and affirmed.

Different Learners

I recently saw a poster that said, "In a world where you can be anything, be kind." I love this. I'd also like a poster that says, "In a world where you can be anything, be you." There is a lot of pressure to be like everybody else. This pressure kicks in intensely in middle school and, in my opin-

---

20 Usain Bolt is a Jamaican runner, a six-time Olympic champion, and frequently named the fastest man in the world.

ion, never goes away completely. That makes it tough for our children who learn (and experience school) differently. We can respond to this pressure with action and love, and give our children strategies to do the same. Figure 24 offers six strategies for social-emotional support. Like much of this book, these suggestions are helpful for all learners. However, for our children who learn differently, these strategies:

> are often overlooked,

> may require more intentionality to put into practice, and

> are vital components of a whole-child support plan.

Peer groups, adult allies, and loving families can step in and show why young people who see the world differently are so important. Yet, even with the most robust social support, difference won't always feel like a gift. As parents, we need to be there with snacks and smiles when our children come home from school and tell us with a disgruntled tone and wounded expression how "everybody else [fill in the blank]."

We need to put down whatever we're doing, sit next to our children, and say, "Tell me what happened."

Then we can listen without correcting, and when the time is right, we can say, "I'm going to let you in on some secrets. Those other kids at school? They're worried about being found out as different, too. We all have unique strengths, challenges, and personalities. Let me tell you some of the things that make you awesome."

Twice-Exceptional Learners

Twice-exceptional (2e) learners are "gifted children who, have the characteristics of gifted students with the potential for high achievement and give evidence of one or more disabilities as defined by federal or state eligibility criteria" (National Association for Gifted Children, n.d., para. 1). These children are often underrepresented in gifted programs, as they are less likely to be identified for gifted testing, and the assessments used to identify gifted students may be a mismatch for the ways their giftedness presents. If your child is struggling in school (academically or behaviorally) and is also highly perceptive, insightful, and remarkably talented in one or more areas, explore these strengths. Further, learning more about 2e children may be helpful for you.

Asynchrony is often pronounced in 2e children. For example, a 10-year-old 2e child may read at a ninth-grade level, use college-level

Different Learners, Same School Six Strategies for Social-Emotional Support	
Find a friend or peer group	Good friends save our lives again and again. Connecting with a friend or peer group can be transformative to the school experience. Sometimes children connect with a like peer, and sometimes children connect with someone quite different from themselves. All children need a friend who accepts, encourages, and wants to share experiences with them. Make sure your child has time and space to connect with friends, laugh, complain, and talk about kid things together.
Find an adult ally	Identify an adult ally in your child's school experience. This critical person can be any school personnel your child connects with, including a teacher, media specialist, administrative assistant, coach, or paraprofessional. An adult ally makes your child feel safe and valued. This person often sees your child not only for who they are right now, but also for who they might become. Make sure this person is included in decision making about your child's school experience and that your child has easy access to this person throughout the day.
Find a safe space	Often the adult ally and safe space go together, but not always. Find a space at school where your child feels safe, can decompress, and always feels welcome. Sometimes this is the office or classroom of the adult ally. Sometimes this is the media center, counseling office, or front office. Your child should have easy access to this safe space during the school day, particularly during stressed times.
Join an activity	Extracurriculars have been cited as key social-emotional supports for young people, linked to both positive mental health and academic benefits. Find a club, sport, or activity for your child to join. In the elementary years, when fewer school clubs are available, you might have to look to community organizations. For children with developmental disabilities, Special Olympics can provide a wonderful opportunity to explore sports, courage, and camaraderie.

Figure 24. Six strategies for social-emotional support.

Different Learners, Same School Six Strategies for Social-Emotional Support	
Know and celebrate strengths	We all have strengths, talents, and gifts. Make sure your child knows some of the reasons that they are exceptional. Cultivate these strengths and celebrate them by giving space and praise for your child to work on activities in their interest area (e.g., drawing, swimming, computers, singing, etc.).
Focus on the positive	Most of us have to retrain ourselves to focus on the positive, to practice gratitude, to pause and share three (or one!) great things that happened today. Commit to focusing on the positive together. Find reasons to be thankful and happy every day and in as many situations as possible. This doesn't mean ignoring what is wrong or what needs to be processed or addressed; it means being real about life without missing all of the good that is happening, too.

Figure 24. Continued.

vocabulary, and understand advanced geometry concepts, but still make frequent mistakes in basic math calculations, have the fine motor skills (including handwriting) of a second grader, and throw temper tantrums like a preschool student. If you notice a similar pattern of strength and challenge in your own child and wonder about twice-exceptionality, you may want to visit with the gifted education team in your district. In recent years, the research around 2e students has increased, and many gifted education personnel are learning more about this population.

The National Association for Gifted Children (n.d.) pointed to parents as critical advocates for their 2e students, particularly in explaining how they see their child's strengths and interests at home. As you work with your school on a plan for your exceptional child, share what you are seeing and give specific examples of your child's strengths, challenges, interests, and personality. School communities often need help understanding the unique needs of twice-exceptional students, who may present with uneven or asynchronous abilities. In particular, families should work collaboratively with schools to help design support plans that integrate rather than isolate the child's educational needs. In 2e children, giftedness and other exceptionalities (e.g., disabilities) coexist (Willard-Holt & Morrison, 2018).

As we've talked about throughout this book, we want to create support plans that both support the disability area and leverage the student's gifts. With 2e students, these exceptionalities may be even more pronounced.

Twice-exceptional children are often extraordinarily adept at understanding how school meets or doesn't meet their learning needs, as well as how the pressures to be "normal" manifest in their school experience. Ask your child for their perceptions, validate their feelings, and affirm that their experiences are real and sometimes difficult. Strategize together around support plans that consider both academic and social-emotional support. Finding friends, peer groups, and safe spaces can be more challenging for 2e students, which means that we must be even more vigilant in seeking out these resources. Twice-exceptional students often connect with their gifted peers in one area (e.g., playing chess, coding a video game, taking an advanced math class) and with their peers with disabilities in another area (e.g., study skills, testing support, and the need for quiet spaces in school). Twice-exceptional children are extremely interesting and often misunderstood. Your love, high expectations, and understanding of these bright children are essential in helping them find both challenge and acceptance at school.

English Language Learners

English language learners (ELLs) bring important global perspectives and may face additional challenges in U.S. public schools. Typically, when a student arrives at school with limited English, schools address the English language needs first. Just as special education services can vary from school to school, so do supports for ELLs. If you are new to the U.S. or the U.S. public school system, are navigating supports for ELLs, and now also suspect your child may have a disability, I just want to pause and acknowledge that this is a lot to manage. Please don't be worried about asking for help from the school, a friend or neighbor, or a local organization serving international groups. Further, schools are required to "communicate information to limited English proficient parents in a language they can understand about any program, service, or activity that is called to the attention of parents who are proficient in English" (U.S. Department of Justice & U.S. Department of Education, 2015, p. 1). If you need translation services, ask your child's school or district to provide those.

Just as the gifted department may be a good starting place for exploring 2e identification (described in the previous section), your child's English as a second language (ESL) or English language learning department is a good starting place for exploring how language learning and a disability may or may not be impacting your child's learning. Generally, schools first want to be sure your child is getting supports to improve in English. Although children tend to acquire language much faster than adults, it takes time to master a new language. Therefore, the school may look at how your child is progressing compared to other ELLs who have had approximately the same level of support. An adjustment period is perfectly normal. The school may also ask you questions about what challenges or struggles you notice when your child is working and learning in their home language. Disabilities are present across languages. You know your child best. If you believe your child would benefit from a special education evaluation, ask for one.

All children are entitled to a quality education, which includes addressing language and learning needs. The year 1974 marked two important legislative acts that continue to guide equal access for English language learners. The first was the court case *Lau v. Nichols*, which affirmed the rights of all children to access an equal education, regardless of native language. The decision went further, saying that equal access included services to support language learning if needed. Soon after, Congress passed the Equal Educational Opportunities Act (EEOA), mandating that no state shall deny equal education opportunity to any individual "by the failure by an educational agency to take appropriate action to overcome language barriers that impede equal participation by students in an instructional program." English language learners are a fast-growing population in U.S. public schools. The perspectives, experiences, and friendships of children from diverse backgrounds make our schools and communities stronger.

Disproportionality

Disproportionality refers to the overrepresentation of culturally and linguistically diverse (CLD) students in special education services and the underrepresentation of CLD students in gifted and advanced services. According to Rebora (2011),

> Federal data from 2007 show that African-American students made up 17 percent of the U.S. school enrollment but more than 20 percent of the students classified with specific learning disabilities. Likewise, Hispanic students

represented just over 20 percent of the school population
but almost 24 percent of students classified with learning
disabilities. (para. 2)

Although these percentage differences may not seem huge, a policy
brief by the National Education Association (NEA, 2008) added that not
only are culturally and linguistically diverse students overidentified for
special education, but they are also often placed in more restrictive environments, receive harsher consequences for behaviors, and may be identified with more profound cognitive, emotional, or behavioral disabilities.
English language learners (especially in districts with lower populations of
ELLs), African American students, and indigenous or Native students are
the most at risk for these classifications.

As the parent of an African American son and as an advocate for
equity in schools, my feelings around disproportionality are personally
complicated and emotionally charged. Throughout his career in K–12
schools, our son was identified in four distinctly different disability categories. Although I believe that ability is malleable, this seems to suggest that
at various times schools weren't sure what was going on with our son. Was
this because he is a complex individual with coexisting strengths and challenges? In part, yes. Could this also have something to do with bias around
race, culture, behavior, and disability? This seems possible. As a family
advocate, I often had to step in and fill the gaps, remind school teams of
his many strengths and talents, get people laughing about his bright personality, and frequently suggest that we hold him to higher expectations.
The privilege of my extensive background in special education policy and
educational rights isn't lost on me. Yet, even with this background, I still
frequently felt confused and disempowered. Navigating special education
services is challenging; adding in the complexities of culture, race, class,
and gender complicates this work further. If something doesn't feel true or
fair, explore that feeling. Ask questions. Reach out to others for help and
advocate with love and high expectations.

Our son needed the services and accommodations on his IEP. That
said, it seemed that important pieces of his story were often missing from
the IEP conversation. Regardless of whether this was about race, ethnicity,
or ability/disability, it was important that someone filled in those gaps. At
times this person was me, and at times this was a compassionate case manager or another critical person in his life (for more info on critical persons,
see pp. 91–92).

Knowing about the history of disproportionately is important, particularly if you are a family of color or raising a child of color. Use this information to ask good questions about your child's learning and behavior, to proceed cautiously and thoughtfully, and above all, to trust your instincts about your child. Working with the school around ability/disability conversations, taking a strengths-based approach, and advancing representative or culturally responsive models[21] are important practices for all children; for kids of color, these practices may also help address larger issues of disproportionality.

As we aim to design a more inclusive world, we must be vigilant in advocating for equity, thoughtful about representation in schools, and persistent in advancing strengths-based conversations about our children.

Designing a More Inclusive World

Family advocates strive to make sure that their children are included in school and that they feel safe, challenged, affirmed, and able to grow and learn. In this book, I have shared many suggestions of ways to think through accommodations and supports when your child learns differently, especially when the existing school structure is a mismatch for your child's exceptionalities. Although individualized accommodations will always be important, there are also some broader ideas about how we can normalize access and difference. In particular, I want to share some brief background on Universal Design for Learning. Knowing that family advocates are critical in disability-rights movements, I think this information is helpful as we imagine a more accessible and inclusive world for our children.

Universal Design for Learning (UDL) or *Universal Design for Instruction* (UDI) is an approach to reconsider access in teaching and learning. UDL extends the work of universal design in architecture, which works to create buildings, products, and spaces that can be used by all people to the greatest extent possible. Consider how automatic doors, ramps, adaptive lighting, and no-slip floors make spaces more accessible for people with physical disabilities as well as parents pushing strollers, professionals with their arms full, and anyone walking across the building with wet shoes.

---

21 *Cultural responsiveness* refers to practices that affirm and recognize the diverse cultures, behaviors, values, and traditions present in our schools.

UDL translates and extends these principles in two key ways: "First, it applies the idea of built-in flexibility to the educational curriculum. Second, it pushes universal design one step further by supporting not only improved access to information within classrooms, but also improved access to learning" (Rose, Meyer, Strangman, & Rappolt, 2002). UDL was created specifically to meet the diverse learning needs of students with disabilities, and it also offers important learning advantages for all students.

The three key principles of UDL, as described by the American Speech-Language-Hearing Association (n.d.), include:
>   presentation of information (e.g., audio support for text, captions for media),
>   expression (e.g., writing, speaking, drawing, and access to assistive technology as needed), and
>   engagement (e.g., choice of tools, adjustable levels of challenge, cognitive supports, and varied groupings).

In planning a UDL lesson, the teacher doesn't include or suggest diversity in presentation, expression, and engagement only for children with disabilities. Instead these considerations are part of the lesson planning and made available to all students. Learning happens when students can both access information and extend that information in meaningful ways. To this end, UDL lessons should not decrease rigor or challenge. We aren't trying to help students get from point A to point B as quickly as possible. Instead, we are trying to make rigor, challenge, process, and learning more accessible to all learners (Rose et al., 2002). In other words, we are trying to get students from their point A to point B (or their point B) as meaningfully as possible.

As the parent of someone who learns differently, you often bring a unique perspective to access and inclusion. You can see how systems, lessons, and environments would or wouldn't work for your child. Sharing this perspective and advocating for greater access and inclusion makes your schools and programs stronger. UDL is one example of this. Look for classrooms (and extracurriculars) that are adopting universal learning principles, acknowledge and appreciate these strategies when you see them in your child's school day, ask for more of these strategies, and brainstorm how your child's school and community can be more inclusive and accessible for all.

Being on a journey is a frequent metaphor in this book. In these chapters, we've talked about reading, learning, and life as journeys. As parents of children who learn differently, we are privileged to be on this nonlinear journey with young people who don't learn or think in the ways their peers do. We get to join them as they find their way, and we can do our best not to miss those moments of creativity, clarity, and inspiration along the way. These moments are always there, even when they are hiding in the pressures of adolescence. As advocates for exceptional children who learn differently, we can commit to valuing the multiple perspectives of our neurodiverse communities. Where is the best place to start? How about starting with the young person right there in front of you, the one asking (in their own way) for you pay attention?

Part IV

Giving Yourself Grace

Grace sounds soft, but it's often a hard lesson to learn, particularly when we're talking about ourselves:

> Parenting is about caretaking. Take care of yourself, too.
> Practice courage.
> Make time for community.
> Remember every day that the best we can do is the best we can do.
> All of your feelings are valid.
> Celebrate the good.

Chapter 8

The (Extra)ordinary Adventure of Raising Different Learners

You are doing important work raising an exceptional child. This is a great adventure. *Great* is a common adjective with a dual meaning: First, it refers to size, specifically "large" in measure and magnitude; second, it refers to being full of emotion. It is no surprise that parenting journeys are marked by a great array of feelings, victories, and many of our most personal challenges. How can we, as parents, navigate this (extra)ordinary adventure of raising different learners? This is a big question, and it is one that I am sure drew you to this book.

In fact, maybe you scanned the Reader's Guide in the Introduction and flipped here immediately. If so, this is a good place to start. If you are arriving here after reading the previous seven chapters, I hope they have helped you with guidance, information, and support around special education services, advocating for your children, and affirming their many strengths. Chapter 8 is meant to support someone else in your child's life—you!

Those of us raising children need support, too. In writing this book, processing my own challenges, and visiting with families who care for children who learn differently, I saw over and over how this journey can be scary, lonely, and exhausting. Yes, of course, there are also great moments of joy and pride. We hold on to these moments, as well we should. We share these moments, too, or versions of them that we think others might understand. However, through this project, I've seen how deeply we hold on to the tough stuff—the loneliness, the fear, and the exhaustion. Many of us (including me) tuck those feelings away, thinking that maybe we'll deal with them later alone (or better yet, not at all). I had heart-to-heart conversations with families who told me they knew that masking the hard stuff wasn't a great idea, but they were busy or didn't know how to process these feelings, so it seemed easier to "just let them be."

Even as I am offering a different approach, I understand how hard it is. Recently, I was talking with a friend and admitted, "Chris and I didn't really talk in real ways to other parents or friends about those [hard] feelings. We should have. I wish someone who cared for us would have said, 'You're not alone. This is hard. Remember, though, you are raising an amazing kid. That said, a lot of days aren't going to feel amazing. Hang in there. I'm there for you.'"

And so, I wrote this book with the hope and encouragement I wish someone had given my family. If you use this guidance, will every day feel great? Nope. Remember, caring for children is about the long game. Often for our children who learn differently, that game feels particularly long. Although there is heartbreak, struggle, and challenge, you and your child are on a great journey together. This journey is marked by love and count-less reasons to celebrate. Every day we get to try to choose gratitude and courage. Look around you; I hope you see friends and family who love you. These people matter. On the days when you fall short, which we all do, call those friends and meet for drinks and dinner, ask your sister to take a walk, cozy up with your partner to watch a movie, and remind yourself that tomorrow will be better.

Like most of the suggestions in these pages, giving yourself grace takes courage. In this last chapter, I'll share personal stories, offer humble advice about navigating your parenting journey, affirm your role as a family advo-cate, and remind you to practice self-care.

Different From Whom?

I am fortunate to have a small group of close friends, most of whom are parents. This community continues to be one of my most important supports. As an academic researcher, I've explored the critical role that community and connections have on students' well-being (Fishman-Weaver, 2018a, 2018b). In the past few years, I've seen how this is also true for parents. After my friend Ann reached out on social media and Chris encouraged me to write this book, I knew that next I would want to run the idea by some of my trusted friends. One afternoon Kay and Sarah, two of my close friends, were at my house. As usual, we were standing in the kitchen making food. It was a cool fall day, and we were fussing over a cheese and tomato soup that didn't really require that much attention.

Hesitatingly I said, "Hey, I have a new idea. . . ." In a single breath I told my friends all about Ann (how brave she was for reaching out), the book I wanted to give to Ann that didn't exist (about parenting children who learn differently and navigating special education services with love and high expectations), and why I thought I should write it (well, actually, this is the part I was looking for encouragement on). Kay, who was stirring our soup, considered. She is the parent of three strong-willed children; her oldest is gender expansive. Sara was cutting bread. She is also a parent of three. At the time, her daughters were working through separate mental health challenges. My friends nodded and encouraged me to go on.

Then, before I could, Kay interrupted me. She stopped stirring the soup that didn't really need her attention, pointed the large spoon at me and said, "Yes! But don't just stop with children with disabilities and their parents. Think about [my child]!" She was getting more excited. "Think about the other stories you could tell. Kathryn, you know this. You could write about being a transracial adoptive family. There are many ways to be different."

I looked at my wise friends. I thought of their children, whom I love, and realized that as usual, my friends were right. We sat down on my back deck with our bread and soup. What followed was a vulnerable and real conversation that has stayed in my head throughout the writing of this book. Each of us shared examples of how our children are different from their peers. We all had deep worries about how school was or wasn't meeting their needs. And each of us said that despite having our supportive friend group, we still often felt alone as parents. Who could possibly understand the unique experiences of our children?

"Different from whom?" is an important question that I have come back to throughout this book. Here we are in the last chapter, and I am still wrestling with it. This book has focused on children whose educational needs include services, accommodations, or modifications outside of the typical differentiation of the general education classroom. Is this limited? You bet. Does this guidance around love, high expectations, and self-care apply to a broader population of children and families? Absolutely! In fact, as more families heard about this project and shared their stories with me—stories of children who receive special education services and stories of children who don't—I realized how universal worry and advocacy are to all parenting. Raising a child who learns differently is hard. Is it harder than raising a child whose idiosyncrasies manifest differently? I think of Kay and Sarah, and I feel pretty sure there's nothing to be gained by making these kinds of comparisons about who has it harder. Instead, there is everything to be gained by acknowledging that all parenting is challenging and we're in this together.

Parenting Is Emotional

Whether you grow your family through birth, marriage, or adoption, the worrying starts the moment you find out you are going to be a parent, and it never stops. Will my child be healthy and happy? Will he be successful? Will she have friends? Will he be kind? You worry about your own ability, too. How will I keep my daughter healthy? What will I do when my son comes home from school crying? What does it mean to be successful? How can I help my children make friends? How can I show them how to be kind? Will I be a good mom, dad, or grandma? What if I don't know what I am doing?

Adding the complexities of disabilities and differences multiplies these worries. What does all of this information about services mean? What do I need to know about our rights? How will I navigate this? There are a million "what ifs" along the parenting journey, constant worries, and plenty of insecurities. Here is a secret, though, and it is one we don't talk about enough: *None of us know what we are doing*. It doesn't matter if you have an advanced degree or if you struggled all of the way through school[22]. It doesn't matter if you have seven kids or one. We're all just doing the best we can and figuring out this parent thing day by day. As you do, there's no appropriate or "normal" way to feel. You have a right to all of the feelings in the human experience. You have a right to be angry, to grieve, and to worry (constantly). You have a right to be relieved, proud, and forever grateful to specific individuals who see your child for who they truly are right now and for who they could be. You will feel many strong emotions

---

22 After reading this book, it should be no surprise that academic struggles and advanced degrees are in no way mutually exclusive. I have dear friends who struggled in school, were identified with disabilities, had IEPs, and have gone on to earn Ph.D.s and become leaders in their communities. These friends found that when it came to parenting, they, too, were making it up as they went along.

during your parenting journey—sometimes you may even feel competing emotions simultaneously.

What should you do with all of these feelings? Name them, own them, and talk about them—all of the things most of us don't do enough. Just as we teach children, naming our emotions helps give us control over them. Hiding our emotions gives them control over us. Give yourself permission to feel whatever emotions come to the surface. If you are feeling lonely, explore that loneliness. Talk about it with someone you trust (e.g., your partner, a close friend, a religious leader). Identifying a small group of people you can reach out to and share with is a powerful act of self-care. You will be a more effective parent and advocate for leaning into your emotions and processing them.

Let's be clear though—this doesn't mean you have to (or even should) answer every curious person's questions about your child. Your child's story is your child's story. Although you are an essential part of that story, some details belong to only you and your family. Likewise, your story is your story. Trust your instincts. If you can, find a small group of people you're comfortable processing with and share with them, commiserate with them, and celebrate with them. Know that this doesn't mean you are under any obligation to broadcast your story to everyone who asks. If someone asks a question that doesn't feel right, don't answer it. Social scripts work for adults, too. I had some common lines I leaned on when strangers ask questions about how school was going. They went something like this:

> "We're finding our way."
> "He's a third grader. We're super into dinosaurs and trains right now."
> "She's got a great teacher—what a blessing."

I kept these social scripts ready for when my instincts told me this was a time to keep it simple.

When you have strong feelings about your child's behaviors, disabilities, or needs (and you will!), you can be candid with yourself and with your close group of trusted friends. At home, though, with your child, be sensitive in how you talk about your feelings. Your children should know that you also experience a range of emotions. However, when you share your feelings with them, do so in a way that is developmentally appropriate and empathetic to their feelings. Most importantly, children should always know that although their disability may be an important part of their identity, it does not define them. No matter what strong emotions are swirling up for you, do your best to consistently remind your child that they are loved, valued, and that you are in this together.

The Great Adventure of Parenting Young Children

My colleagues and I were deeply engaged in a conversation about lesson plans when a woman interrupted us.

"Excuse me," she said, "I am a new mom."

We were working at a crowded café during our lunch hour. We looked up, a bit surprised by this introduction. Sensing our surprise, the new mom held up her empty fountain cup as a kind of explanation. "Would you watch my baby for a minute while I go fill up my soda? I'm still figuring . . ." she gestured to a large stroller, ". . . all of this out. I heard you all talking about school, so I thought you were probably safe. I don't want you to think I would leave him with just anybody!" She looked tired in a way that was extremely familiar.

"Of course!" we answered nearly in unison.

"Take your time getting your soda!" one of my colleagues encouraged. "Use it as a mini-vacation."

The new mother smiled meekly and wheeled up a tiny sleeping babe who was wrapped in several blankets and fast asleep in an enormous stroller. Being a new parent is terrifying—and beautiful. Often we're so overwhelmed with the responsibility and exhausted from lack of sleep, that it's hard to remember to see the beauty. I watched this small child sleeping in his stroller and thought of my own children. The baby's chest rose and fell so slightly under the blanket that I had to concentrate not to miss it. I've often wondered how many times I have watched my own children sleeping. It's still almost a ritual to tiptoe into my daughter's room, to find my way in the shadows, to wait for my eyes to adjust until her sweet face comes into focus, and to listen until I hear the small even sound of her breathing. Across the café this baby's tired mother was filling her plastic cup with Dr Pepper. Although I didn't know anything about either them, I suddenly felt very connected to both the mom and son. I was also glad that she had been brave enough to walk up to three strangers and ask for a couple minutes of help. We don't do that enough.

The more I learn about parenting, the more convinced I am that we're all making this up as we go along. Think about the moment when a new child was placed in your arms. It didn't matter how much you had read and prepared (or hadn't); you looked at that sweet face and had no idea what you were doing.

In almost no time at all, the new mom came back and thanked us. She wheeled her son back to their table, sipped her soda, and ate a few bites of a blueberry muffin. Before she'd finished the muffin or the soda, her son woke up hungry and ready for attention.

The Great Adventure of Parenting Teenage Children

When our son crossed the stage at his high school graduation, my husband squeezed my hand, and I whispered, "He did it."

Our extended family was seated around us. They cheered, hollered, and patted us vigorously on the back. "Congratulations," they said. "You two did it."

Both statements are true. We all did it. Raising a child takes a community.

High school graduation is always a cause for celebration. However, for children who learn differently, the journey to cross that stage is often marked by different uncertainties than their grade-level peers experience. As parents, this can be an isolating experience. Often it feels like everyone else's family views a 4-year college as a foregone conclusion. Many parents of children with disabilities aren't sure if or when their child will graduate high school, and they are scared and uncertain about what will happen next.

Coming of age is a cacophony of emotion for everyone. Adolescence plus asynchrony can lead to remarkable moments of glimpsing the adult your child is becoming. These moments are often fleeting and followed by huge reminders of the children they very much still are and (of course) no longer think of themselves as. I recommend keeping chocolate on hand for everyone involved. Middle school and high school are complicated and important times for development. These years are often made more complex by your child's differences. Remember the deep pressure to be like everyone else that kicks in around middle school? If not, your teenager will remind you when she arrives home hurt and confused, followed by slammed doors, tearing into a package of cookies, tears, and not wanting to talk about it. When these things make you want to storm into school, or when you want to tell your child they are being ridiculous—pause. Listen. Try to remember yourself as a teenager. Then tell yourself that, even at your very best perspective-taking moments, you still can't know exactly what is like to be the kid your child is.

Often it helps to think about where your child was 5 or 10 years ago. Sometimes it's hard to see the progress when you're in the thick of it every day. Zoom out, and usually there is a lot to celebrate. Hold on to those breakthrough moments. Notice the dreams your child is choosing to chase. And if you still feel like storming into school, call a friend and talk it through first.

The Importance of Community

I recently completed a longitudinal study on the social-emotional needs of high-achieving young women (Fishman-Weaver, 2018b). I planned focus groups, guest speakers, interviews, and a host of special events to explore the topic. At the end of the multiyear study, I asked each participant what her biggest takeaway was. Unanimously every woman said that belonging to the group was her most significant outcome. Years of research, and what mattered most was that the students felt *included* in a group. Good friends save our lives over and over again.

Yet, we often miss just how important friendship is. We all need people we can connect with, laugh with, and be ourselves with. Like other relationships, friendships have to be nurtured. Once you become a parent, there isn't a lot of encouragement to pour into these relationships. In fact, sometimes parents (particularly mothers) receive messages that making time for friends means taking time off from parenting. I have heard from many mothers who, while out with their friends, had someone say to them, "Oh, how nice you got a break. Is your husband babysitting the kids?" No, he's not babysitting—he's parenting! We have to stop doing this to each other. Parenting is hard enough without constructing arbitrary pressures to do so alone.

Raising a child who learns differently is often a lonely experience, but going it alone isn't healthy for families or communities. More than 2,000 years ago, Aristotle remarked that humans are social animals. So are parents. This chapter is a call to reframe parenting (and living) as a community experience.

Just as the participants in my last study said that belonging to a group of like-peers was transformative for them, just as we know classroom community is essential for our students, having a group of friends is essential for you, too. Parenting is exhausting and deeply rewarding. Parenting a child who learns differently can feel all-consuming. Finding appropriate care, wondering how long you have until the phone rings with a call from school, and quieting the worry long enough to engage with another adult are real challenges to connection. I am not minimizing those challenges; instead, I am saying that they are worth working through. When someone asks you to happy hour, when you want to join that book club, when your partner suggests a date, or when the neighbor says, "Let's try a playdate," don't make your default, "no thanks." I know all of the reasons to talk yourself out of it—you don't feel like you have anything in common with the group at happy hour, you don't have time to read the book club book, you don't know who could watch your child, and the neighbor won't understand your child's needs. The list goes on. I know these reasons, because these are the things I told myself. Looking back, I wish I hadn't. This book is an opportunity for me to share some things I wish someone had told me. Next time you start talking yourself out of connecting, pause and ask, "What if this time I made it work? What if this time I surprised myself and said yes?"

Raising children, including children who learn differently, can happen within the context of community. Who do you call when you have great news? Who do you reach out to when you're crying and unsure what to do next? Those are the relationships you want to nurture. Those are the people you can text in desperation and say, "Would you come over?" And when they do, give them your kids for 20 minutes so you can take a shower and maybe even drink a cup of coffee while it is still hot.

If you have a partner, nurture that relationship[23]. Without intentionality, the windstorm of raising a child who learns differently can take over everything. There will be times when you will disagree on services, discipline, expectations, and advocacy approaches. Try to talk it through, and remember that "talking it through" almost always means more listening

---

23 I know not everyone reading this book has a partner. Some of you are raising children on your own. I see you and am sending you love (because friends send love). This journey is challenging, and you are doing a great job. This journey can also be isolating; find a community, or even just one dear friend, and call those people when you need a laugh or a listening ear.

than talking. Sometimes you'll compromise. Other times, you'll have to agree to disagree. It's not easy. The only person who knows your child as well as you is your partner. And that person is likely just as invested as you.

The stakes are high. Both you and your partner will feel all of those big raw emotions, and because you are different people, you will process them differently. I don't think it's possible to coparent a child who learns differently without having several opportunities to say you're sorry. When you lose your temper, when you can't listen right now, or when you miss something, apologize and remind each other that you're in this together. Your child is worth fighting for—so are you, and so is your marriage or relationship.

Find a sitter who will keep your children safe so you can go on a date. It doesn't even matter what you do when you go on that date. Personally, some of my best dates with my husband have included the bliss of grocery shopping without chasing a child down the aisles. And when/if the needs of your child are such that a date out isn't possible, have a "home date." My family started this tradition when our son was young, because it was what worked for us. After we got our son to bed, we'd make a cheese plate, pour a glass of wine, watch a movie, or play Scrabble. We planned home dates in advance so that we could look forward to the time to connect with each other. These moments—and often they are only moments before you get interrupted—give you strength to tackle the whirlwind of parenting. Sometimes when raising a child who learns differently, it feels like you are surviving in Tornado Alley. In those moments, weeks, and years, hold fast to each other.

The Importance of Self-Care

Parenting is one of the hardest things I've ever done (am still doing). When it gets hard, I hope we can be brave enough to listen to our emotions, to ask for what we need, and then to look for reasons to be grateful (they are always there). While doing so, let's give ourselves grace. *Grace* sounds soft, but it's a hard lesson to learn, particularly when we're talking about ourselves.

While writing this book, I talked with several families whose children have now grown up. Revisiting the IEP years was often painful. Remembering these moments brought up some of our most difficult memories. We talked about guilt, shame, frustration, and sadness. At the same time, we shared stories about what our children were doing now and how we were proud of the people they were continuing to become. All of us, me included, shared that if we had it to do over again, we would make different choices. This was a difficult admission that was frequently met with tears. Even as I felt it, something about this idea seemed unsettling to me. Without getting too metaphysical, if I had to navigate this experience again, neither my son nor or I would be the same people. All we can do in any given moment is the best we know how to do.

Occasionally, I still stay up thinking about different services that might have helped, different ways I could have handled conversations, and different advocacy approaches my family might have taken. When you love someone, when you invest in that person, and when you see yourself in your child, the stakes are unbelievably high. Sometimes things don't go as planned. Sometimes we fall short. And because we don't talk about these feelings enough to normalize them, they live deep in the silence of our souls. Let's break this silence. Are you replaying IEP meetings, wishing you had chosen another service plan or school, thinking about how you could have handled a certain conversation differently? Feel those emotions and then talk to your partner or friend. Afterward, do your best to let the past go and to keep moving forward.

I recently spoke at a leadership conference. A theme of the conference—which included health workers, family counselors, and other caregivers—was that we can't care as effectively for others if we aren't also caring for ourselves. Like making space for friendship, we rarely give ourselves permission to prioritize self-care, ask for help, or practice courage. This section isn't a recipe for self-care. Self-care, especially self-care for parents, can look like many things. Sometimes it's drinking 65 ounces of water a day, and other times it's meeting friends for a drink. Sometimes it's taking a fitness class, and other times it's wearing pajamas and watching Netflix. Sometimes it means choosing a protein bar, and other times it means enjoying that candy bar. It all comes back to a central question: *How are you taking care of yourself?* If the answer is "I'm not," stop and ask yourself what you need right now. Maybe it *is* a big glass of water. Or maybe it's a 5-minute break to walk around the block. Parenting has always been about caregiving. Care for yourself, too.

The Importance of Courage

Courage is the connection between strength and vulnerability. It's the practice of doing that thing that our heart says is right and our brain says is going to be hard (Fishman-Weaver, 2018b). This book was inspired by a courageous call for help from my friend Ann. Her call inspired me to take a leap of faith and write this book.

I wondered, could my experiences offer some guidance, comfort, and wisdom to others? Even though my confidence was shaky, I started writing. And then, halfway through drafting this manuscript, I almost gave up. My self-talk sounded something like this: *Who am I to write this book? Shouldn't I be a perfect parent to write a book for other parents?* Suddenly I was overwhelmed with all of the things I was still figuring out. What gifts could I possibly give to other families?

I tried to take some of my own advice. I took a long walk. I had a good cry (okay, a dozen). I took a nap. I reread work I was proud of. I ate dark chocolate. I went to church. Slowly, with the encouragement of friends and family, some of whom knew more about my family's story than others, I started writing again. I shared the first half of this book with Ann. And guess what? The chapters helped her. She told me that she went into her next IEP meeting more confident than ever. She said she felt heard, hopeful, and more ready to advocate with love for her son.

Something I had written at the beginning of this project caught my attention: *Honesty is one of the most inspiring gifts you can give.* Suddenly, this felt true and relevant. I am not a perfect parent, and that's okay because the perfect parent is a myth. All of us—children and families alike—are works in progress. I don't have to have everything figured out to have something valid and important to offer. The same is true for you.

The more we can practice courageous disclosure, the more we can allow ourselves to show up saying, "Here is what I know, and here is what I am still figuring out," the more we can reach out to someone and ask, "Do you have a few minutes?", and the more I believe our communities will shift to places of courage, connection, and self-care. Honesty is courage. Friendship is courage. Asking for help is courage.

Working on this book taught me just how deep the need for emotional strength and honest disclosure (two big courage indicators) are when tackling this parenting adventure. Parenting is challenging; parenting a child who learns differently is (extra)ordinarily challenging. Courage requires us to walk into the difficult meeting, to stand up to injustice, or to tell someone we trust, "Hey, I need some help with this."

With parenting, we rarely get to choose our challenges. Often they are handed to us, and the only choice we have is how to respond. Sometimes really difficult things are outside of our sphere of influence. Over the past several chapters, we've talked through practical strategies, policy information, and special education jargon. This information is important. However, my true hopes for this book are bigger than any of those details.

I hope I have given you honesty, friendship, and encouragement. I hope you are walking away more willing to ask for help and more confident in advocating for your child. Take a few minutes today to look at your beautiful, imperfect, idiosyncratic family. Really look. You can acknowledge that, yes, this journey is difficult and also that there is nothing more important. If you only remember one thing when you close this book, remember that love is the most important force in raising children (and parents, too).

References

Ackerman, C. (2018). Self-fulfilling prophecy in psychology: 10 examples and definition. *Positive Psychology Program*. Retrieved from https://positivepsychologyprogram.com/self-fulfilling-prophecy

ADA National Network. (2019). *What is the definition of disability under the ADA?* Retrieved from https://adata.org/faq/what-definition-disability-under-ada

AdoptUSKids. (n.d.). *Adopt the children*. Retrieved from https://www.adoptuskids.org/meet-the-children/children-in-foster-care/about-the-children

American Speech-Language-Hearing Association. (n.d.). *Universal design for learning*. Retrieved from https://www.asha.org/SLP/schools/Universal-Design-for-Learning

Americans with Disabilities Act, 42 U.S.C. §§ 12102 et seq. (1990).

Anderson, M. (2016). *Learning to choose, choosing to learn: The key to student motivation and achievement*. Alexandria, VA: ASCD.

Armstrong, T. (2015). The myth of the normal brain: Embracing neurodiversity. *AMA Journal of Ethics, 17*, 348–352.

Austin, R. D., & Pisano, G. P. (2017). Neurodiversity as a competitive advantage. *Harvard Business Review*. Retrieved from https://hbr.org/2017/05/neurodiversity-as-a-competitive-advantage

Brown v. Board of Education of Topeka, 347 U.S. 483 (1954).

Carroll, L. (1871). *Jabberwocky*. Retrieved from https://www.poetryfoundation.org/poems/42916/jabberwocky

Crespi, B. J. (2016). Autism as a disorder of high intelligence. *Frontiers in Neuroscience, 10*, 300.

Disability Rights Education and Defense Fund. (n.d.). *Section 504 of the Rehabilitation Act of 1973*. Retrieved from https://dredf.org/legal-advocacy/laws/section-504-of-the-rehabilitation-act-of-1973

Doidge, N. (2016). *The brain's way of healing: Remarkable discoveries and recoveries from the frontiers of neuroplasticity* (Updated ed.). New York, NY: Penguin.

Dweck, C. (2006). *Mindset: The new psychology of success*. New York, NY: Ballantine Books.

Economic Opportunities Amendments of 1972, Pub. Law 92-424 (September 19, 1972).

Education for All Handicapped Children Act of 1975, Pub. Law 94-142 (November 29, 1975).

Edwards, S. (2019). Reading and the brain. *On the Brain: The Harvard Mahoney Neuroscience Institute Letter*. Retrieved from https://neuro.hms.harvard.edu/harvard-mahoney-neuroscience-institute/brain-newsletter/and-brain-series/reading-and-brain

Elementary and Secondary Education Act of 1965, §142, 20 U.S.C. 863.

Equal Educational Opportunities Act of 1974, 20 U.S.C. §§ 1701–1758 (1974).

Family Educational Rights and Privacy Act, 20 U.S.C. § 1232g.

Fishman-Weaver, K. (2018a, March). School as a community project. *Principal Leadership, 18*. Retrieved from https://www.nassp.org/category/pl/volume-18-2017-2018/page/12

Fishman-Weaver, K. (2018b). *Wholehearted teaching of gifted young women: Cultivating courage, connection, and self-care in schools*. Waco, TX: Prufrock Press.

Florida Department of Education. (2019). *ESE eligibility*. Retrieved from http://www.fldoe.org/academics/exceptional-student-edu/ese-eligibility

Folkins, J. (1992). Resource on person-first language: The language used to describe individuals with disabilities. *American Speech-Language-Hearing Association*. Retrieved from https://hksnyder.weebly.com/uploads/4/2/5/0/42509269/resource_on_person-first_language.pdf

Freeman, D. (2005) *Corduroy goes to the doctor*. New York, NY: Viking Books for Young Readers.

Gittings, P. (2013). Blind runner beats poverty, bullies to become champion. *CNN*. Retrieved from https://www.cnn.com/2013/02/20/sport/brazil-terezinha-guilhermina-paralympics/index.html

Grandin, T. (2006). *Thinking in pictures: My life with autism* (Expanded ed.). New York, NY: Vintage Books.

Handicapped Children's Early Education Assistance Act of 1968, Pub. Law 90-538 (September 30, 1968).

Hartnett, D. N., Nelson, J. M., & Rinn, A. N. (2004). Gifted or ADHD? The possibilities of misdiagnosis. *Roeper Review, 26,* 73–76.

Heasley, S. (2015). Target ad includes model with disability. *Disability Scoop.* Retrieved from https://www.disabilityscoop.com/2015/10/27/target-ad-model-disability/20905

Honos-Webb, L. (2010). *The gift of ADHD: How to transform your child's problems into strengths* (2nd ed.). Oakland, CA: New Harbinger.

Howard, V. (2011). The importance of pleasure reading in the lives of young teens: Self-identification, self-construction and self-awareness. *Journal of Librarianship and Information Science, 43,* 46–55.

Individuals with Disabilities Education Act, 20 U.S.C. §1401 et seq. (1990).

Individuals with Disabilities Education Improvement Act, Pub. Law 108-446 (December 3, 2004).

Invisible Disabilities Association. (n.d.). *How do you define invisible disability?* Retrieved from https://invisibledisabilities.org/what-is-an-invisible-disability

Iuculano, T., Rosenberg-Lee, M., Supekar, K., Lynch, C. J., Khouzam, A., Phillips, J., & Menon, V. (2014). Brain organization underlying superior mathematical abilities in children with autism. *Biological Psychiatry, 75,* 223–230.

John's Crazy Socks. (2019). *John Lee Cronin.* Retrieved from https://johnscrazysocks.com/pages/john-lee-cronin

Konnikova, M. (2015). How children learn to read. *The New Yorker.* Retrieved from https://www.newyorker.com/science/maria-konnikova/how-children-learn-read

Krezmien, M. P., Leone, P. E., & Achilles, G. M. (2006). Suspension, race, and disability: Analysis of statewide practices and reporting. *Journal of Emotional and Behavioral Disorders, 14,* 217–226.

Lau v. Nichols, 414 U.S. 563 (1974).

Lee, A. M. I. (2019). 10 key procedural safeguards in IDEA. *Understood. org.* Retrieved from https://www.understood.org/en/school-learning/your-childs-rights/basics-about-childs-rights/10-key-procedural-safeguards-in-idea

McNabb, L. A. (2016). Reading books, particularly diverse books, is important to health. *National Council of Teachers of English.* Retrieved from https://www2.ncte.org/blog/2016/04/reading-books-particularly-diverse-books-important-health-2

Meyler, A., Keller, T. A., Cherkassky, V. L., Gabrieli, J. D. E., & Just, M. A. (2008). Modifying the brain activation of poor readers during sentence comprehension with extended remedial instruction: A longitudinal study of neuroplasticity. *Neuropsychologia, 46,* 2580–2592.

Mills v. Board of Education of the District of Columbia, 348 F. Supp. 866 (D.D.C. 1972).

Nall, R. (2016). The benefits of ADHD. *Healthline.* Retrieved from https://www.healthline.com/health/adhd/benefits-of-adhd#1

National Association for Gifted Children. (n.d.). *Twice-exceptional students.* Retrieved from https://www.nagc.org/resources-publications/resources-parents/twice-exceptional-students

National Education Association. (2008). *Disproportionality: Inappropriate identification of culturally and linguistically diverse children.* Retrieved from https://www.nea.org/assets/docs/HE/mf_PB02_Disproportionality.pdf

Nicolaidis, C. (2012). What can physicians learn from the neurodiversity movement? *American Medical Association Journal of Ethics, 14,* 503–510.

Oettingen, G. (2014). *Rethinking positive thinking: Inside the new science of motivation.* New York, NY: Current.

Oettingen, G., Mayer, D., Timur Sevincer, A., Stephens, E. J., Pak, H. J., & Hagenah, M. (2009). Mental contrasting and goal commitment: The mediating role of energization. *Personality and Social Psychology Bulletin, 35,* 608–622.

Office for Civil Rights. (2018). *Protecting students with disabilities.* Retrieved from https://www2.ed.gov/about/offices/list/ocr/504faq.html?exp

Office of Special Education and Rehabilitative Services. (2010). *The Office of Special Education and Rehabilitative Services celebrates 35 years of Individuals with Disabilities Education Act (IDEA).* Retrieved from https://www2.ed.gov/about/offices/list/osers/idea35/index.html

Pennsylvania Association for Retarded Citizens v. Commonwealth, 334 F. Supp. 1257 (E.D. Pa. 1971).

Peters, T. (2018). The first Gerber baby with Down syndrome will steal your heart. *Today.* Retrieved from https://www.today.com/parents/2018-gerber-baby-first-gerber-baby-down-syndrome-t122258

Pub. Law 89-313 (November 1, 1965).

Rebora, A. (2011). Keeping special ed in proportion. *Education Week.* Retrieved from https://www.edweek.org/tsb/articles/2011/10/13/01 disproportion.h05.html

Rosa's Law, Pub. Law 111-256 (October 5, 2010).

Rose, D. H., Meyer, A., Strangman, N., & Rappolt, G. (2002). *Teaching every student in the digital age: Universal design for learning.* Alexandria, VA: ASCD.

Scales, P. (2005). *Winning back your reluctant readers.* Retrieved from https://www.randomhouse.com/highschool/RHI_magazine/reluc tant_readers/scales.html

Section 504 of the Rehabilitation Act, 29 U.S.C. Section 706 et. Seq. (1973).

Special Education Guide. (2019). *Specific learning disabilities.* Retrieved from https://www.specialeducationguide.com/disability-profiles/ specific-learning-disabilities

Spread the Word. (2019). *About Spread the Word.* Retrieved from https:// www.spreadtheword.global/about

UnderstandingSpecialEducation.com. (2016). *Understanding the 13 categories of special education.* Retrieved from https://www.understand ingspecialeducation.com/13-categories-of-special-education.html

U.S. Census Bureau. (2012). Nearly 1 in 5 people have a disability in the U.S., census bureau reports. *Newsroom Archive.* Retrieved from https:// www.census.gov/newsroom/releases/archives/miscellaneous/cb12-134.html

U.S. Department of Education. (n.d.). *About IDEA.* Retrieved from https:// sites.ed.gov/idea/about-idea

U.S. Department of Education. (2008). *Twenty-sixth annual report to congress on the implementation of the Individuals with Disabilities Education Act.* Retrieved from https://www2.ed.gov/about/reports/ annual/osep/2004/index.html

U.S. Department of Justice, & U.S. Department of Education. (2015). *Information for limited English proficient (LEP) parents and guardians and for schools and school districts that communicate with them.* Retrieved from https://www2.ed.gov/about/offices/list/ocr/docs/dcl-factsheet-lep-parents-201501.pdf

von Ravensberg, H., & Blakely, A. (2018). When to use functional behavioral assessment? Best practice vs. legal guidance. *Positive Behavioral Interventions and Supports.* Retrieved from https://www.pbis.org/ evaluation/evaluation-briefs/when-to-use-fba

Vygotsky, L. S. (1978). *Mind in society: The development of higher psychological processes.* Cambridge, MA: Harvard University Press.

Willard-Holt, C., & Morrison, K. (2018). Uncovering buried treasure: Effective learning strategies for twice-exceptional students. In C. Danielian, C. M. Fugate, & E. Fogarty (Eds.), *Teaching gifted children: Success strategies for teaching high-ability learners* (pp. 489–494). Waco, TX: Prufrock Press.

Wineburg, S. S. (1987). The self-fulfillment of the self-fulfilling prophecy. *Educational Researcher, 16*(9), 28–37.

The Wrightslaw Way. (2010). *Do I have to sign the IEP?* Retrieved from https://www.wrightslaw.com/blog/do-i-have-to-sign-the-iep

About the Author

Kathryn Fishman-Weaver, Ph.D., is an educator, author, and advocate for student leadership. She has a group of exceptional students in Oakland, CA, to thank for teaching her how to be a teacher. Dr. Fishman-Weaver has used these lessons to teach special education, gifted education, language arts, and teacher preparation. Currently she serves as the Director of Academic Affairs and Engagement for Mizzou Academy where she continues to learn with students and teachers across the globe. Her first book, *Wholehearted Teaching of Gifted Young Women*, has been read and implemented by educators internationally. Dr. Fishman-Weaver loves the smell of old books, the quiet of her back deck, and impromptu family dance parties in her kitchen.